Read with Me

Read with Me

Engaging Your Young Child in Active Reading

Samantha Cleaver
Munro Richardson

ROWMAN & LITTLEFIELD
Lanham • Boulder • New York • London

Published by Rowman & Littlefield
An imprint of The Rowman & Littlefield Publishing Group, Inc.
4501 Forbes Boulevard, Suite 200, Lanham, Maryland 20706
www.rowman.com

6 Tinworth Street, London SE11 5AL

British Library Cataloguing in Publication Information Available

Library of Congress Cataloging-in-Publication Data

Names: Cleaver, Samantha, 1981– author. | Richardson, Munro, 1971– author.
Title: Read with me : engaging your young child in active reading / Samantha Cleaver,
    Munro Richardson.
Description: Lanham : Rowman & Littlefield, 2019. | Includes bibliographical references.
Identifiers: LCCN 2018014484 (print) | LCCN 2018046492 (ebook) |
    ISBN 9781475836714 (ebook) | ISBN 9781475836691 (cloth : alk. paper)
Subjects: LCSH: Reading (Preschool) | Reading comprehension. | Literacy. |
    Active learning.
Classification: LCC LB1140.5.R4 (ebook) | LCC LB1140.5.R4 C53 2019 (print) |
    DDC 372.4—dc23
LC record available at https://lccn.loc.gov/2018014484

To my Active Readers, Saha and Neina.
—Samantha Cleaver

To Teresa, who nurtured a love of reading
in our three bookworms.
—Munro Richardson

Contents

Acknowledgments

This book would not have been possible without the interest, collaboration, and ongoing dedication of many people. First, we would like to thank the parents who committed to do Active Reading with their children and share their experiences and challenges across the Charlotte, North Carolina, community. Our colleagues Ron Fairchild, Jenny Bogoni, and Mike English in the Campaign for Grade Level Reading gave us early encouragement to translate our research findings into workable strategies for families. We would also like to thank the Charlotte Mecklenburg Library for working with us to spread Active Reading to families and organizations, specifically the librarians who provided recommendations and feedback. We're grateful to Charlotte Speech and Hearing for graciously sharing their expertise regarding early language acquisition. Read Charlotte's Active Reading Action Learning Team (you know who you are) helped us learn how Active Reading can be infused into the community. A special thank you to Jay Everett and Kristi Thomas at Wells Fargo for your very early support of Active Reading in Charlotte-Mecklenburg. And, finally, thank you to the Read Charlotte board and team who were committed to the vision and potential of this book for our community and others.

Introduction

The Power of Active Reading

My daughter, Saha, age almost-three, brings me the book *Where the Wild Things Are* by Maurice Sendak. I've lost count of how many times I've read the story of mischievous Max and his "over a year and in and out of weeks" trip to meet the Wild Things. I pull her onto my lap, open the book, and begin to read.

At the start of the story, Max is nailing a homemade tent to a wall and jumping down stairs wielding a fork aimed at his dog.

"Max is being naughty," Saha says.

"That's right," I say and point to the picture of Max jumping down the stairs toward his dog. "He might hurt his dog."

Saha nods.

"What is his mommy going to do?" I ask.

"Time-out," she says.

"That's right; he's going to get a time-out," I say.

We read each page, stopping to talk about how Max's room turns into a forest.

"What is a forest?" I ask.

"Where lots of trees are," she says.

I ask questions about the story: How did Max feel? What did Max and the Wild Things do? Saha answers some of them, and I help her answer other questions.

Saha fills in parts of the story. "And Max said," I read.

"No," Saha says emphatically.

We show each other our "terrible claws" and gnash our "terrible teeth."

At the end of the story, Max arrives home to find his dinner, still hot.

"How do you think Max felt?" I ask.

"Good," she replies.

"That's right; he did feel good," I say. "And Max's mommy must have loved him if his dinner was still hot." I give her a squeeze and she hops down from my lap, scampering off to pull blocks off a shelf.

When Saha and I started reading *Where the Wild Things Are*, she didn't know what it meant to "make mischief" or have "terrible claws." She didn't know what a forest was. She did not understand the significance of the hot dinner on the first reading. And she wasn't able to complete the sentences the first time through. But the more she and I read the book together, the more I asked questions, told her what I saw in the story, and encouraged her conversation, the more she commented on the story and the more she was able to answer. After a few weeks of reading Max's story, Saha connected her naughty behavior with Max's antics, agreeing that both she and Max could make mischief "of one kind or another" and that they deserved a time-out.

Where the Wild Things Are is one of my favorite storybooks to read aloud. Active Reading, the practice of Asking questions, Building vocabulary, and Connecting to the child's world while reading, made the experience that much more powerful for both of us. I saw Saha come to love Max and the Wild Things as much as I did because she connected the story to her own life. I watched her discover new things in the book each time we read. It's one thing to read a book you love to your child; it's another to see them come to love the same book on their own terms.

In addition to being a parent to two young children both under the age of four, I also work with Read Charlotte, a nonprofit organization committed to doubling the percent of third-grade students who read proficiently from 39 percent in 2015 to 80 percent by 2025. This is an important task. Children who read proficiently by the end of third grade are almost destined to graduate high school (96 percent of proficient readers graduate from high school).[1] This remains true for students who face challenges. For example, 89 percent of low-income students who read proficiently by third grade will graduate high school.[2] There are few other factors that we can point to, and that we can influence, that have as great an impact on a child's life than their ability to read well by third grade.

At Read Charlotte, we know that to provide our children with the best start in school, we must build foundational language and literacy skills early. Fortunately, decades of research pointed us to Active Reading, or techniques that adults can do with young children (age two to five) that are easy to incorporate into reading sessions and that have dramatic impacts on a child's language and early literacy skills.

The language and practices of Active Reading were developed from decades of research on other read-aloud approaches (dialogic reading,[3] shared interactive reading[4]) starting in 2016. Active Reading is one of the main initiatives that Read Charlotte is working to spread across Mecklenburg County.

When I started this work, Saha was two, just old enough to start engaging in Active Reading herself. I was a former teacher working toward a PhD in special education with a focus on literacy at the University of North Carolina at Charlotte. The more I read the research, the more I changed how I read with Saha (and, subsequently, her younger sister, Neina). This was shocking to me—I'd taught kids to read and getting my own kids to read was not an aspect of parenting that I was concerned about.

As infants go, Saha had been an avid reader. She sat through stacks of board books as a baby and could entertain herself with books long enough for me to cook dinner. But, while I may have read more books or asked more questions than other caregivers, I was still reading *to* Saha, not reading *with* her. She was my first "case study," and I learned as much from her as I did from the research.

Since starting the work on Active Reading, I have incorporated the ABCs of Active Reading and specific prompts (pointing, fill-in-the-blank, Talk More, questioning) into the reading that we do at home. Saha quickly responded, becoming an avid talker in addition to an avid reader. Her engagement with stories increased, and I started to see the outcomes in the research happening in my own living room as Saha used more words, connected with characters, and asked questions of her own when we read. She eagerly completes stories, reciting the words from memory or telling the story based on the pictures and her memory. Now, at almost four years old, she quickly summarizes stories and makes connections with stories and characters that constantly surprise her father and me.

I really shouldn't be surprised to see the growth in my own daughter. Active Reading practices have been proven to have a strong effect on kids' expressive and receptive language.[5] Essentially, when children are read to using Active Reading techniques, they gain language skills faster than children who aren't exposed to those same techniques. In the long term, this prepares children to be fully engaged readers. Children who regularly experience Active Reading, even just a few times a week, have what it takes to be lifelong lovers of reading and the language and comprehension skills to understand what they read, make new meaning, and connect in relevant ways to text.

At the start of this work, I admit, I thought that pushing parents to read with kids was akin to telling people to brush their teeth twice a day. We all know that reading is good for you and we should all probably read more, but what public campaign was really going to change how parents and teachers read with kids when their days are already full? But it soon became obvious that it was less about getting caregivers to read and more about getting them to shift *how* they read—changing the conversation from reading *to* kids to reading *with* them.

A picture book and a short burst of Active Reading—say fifteen minutes in the lull after dinner and before bedtime—can have a powerful impact. This book is about that shift and I hope it inspires you to make small but important changes in your daily reading routine and to look for the benefits of Active Reading in the children you read with every day.

—Samantha Cleaver

As parents of young children, my wife and I had some fuzzy idea that we were supposed to read to our three girls if we wanted to be good parents. I grew up in a house full of books, was read to constantly as a child, and started kindergarten as a beginning reader. My wife, who immigrated to the United States from Taiwan at age five, was not read to at home and grew up with few age-appropriate books at home. But despite the differences in our childhood experiences, we both wanted books to be a part of our shared family life. So we read to our kids. A lot.

When our girls were very young, my wife, Teresa, took on the lion's share of this job. She read them a wide variety of picture books. Many of these books were classic children's books that have withstood the test of time, like *Where The Wild Things Are* by Maurice Sendak, *The Snowy Day* by Ezra Jack Keats, and *Madeline* by Ludwig Bemelmans. She read books that won various children's books awards (and the runner-ups) over the decades, like *Joseph Had a Little Overcoat* by Simms Taback and *Kitten's Full Moon* and *Julius, Baby of the World* by Kevin Henkes. And she read books whose only award was my children's giggles and laughter, like *A Friend for Dragon* by Dav Pilkey, *The Seven Chinese Sisters* by Kathy Tucker, and *I'd Really Like to Eat a Child* by Sylviane Donnio. My wife didn't just read the words on the page. She acted them out. She read in silly voices. She sang the songs. She stopped and asked questions. The girls loved to correct my wife when she (intentionally) made mistakes or "forgot" words in their favorite books. And she read many of those books over and over and over.

From day one, our girls understood that reading was an activity that Mom and Dad fully supported. And, for our part, we went out of our way to find books that they were interested in. But we didn't have to break our family budget to support our girls' book habit. Our girls knew the children's librarian at our public library on a first-name basis. On Saturdays, we took family trips to a local used bookstore and let them pick out new books to keep. Everyone in our family knew to buy our girls books for their birthdays and holidays. We eventually had so many books in our house that my wife made a rule: for a new book to come into the house, an old book had to go out. We paid it forward by always donating our used children's books to a local nonprofit that provided child-care services to low-income children in our community.

Today, our oldest daughter is in college; the youngest is in middle school. They each have different personalities and interests, but they all love to read. A lot. I don't want to give you the false impression that we did everything right. We made our fair share of mistakes, especially with our oldest. (Sorry, Melina.) Looking back, we got lucky with a number of things, including how we read with our girls. At the time, we had no idea that:

- There is a difference between reading *to* a child and reading *with* them.
- Reading can help build neural pathways in a young child's still-developing brain.
- Reading children's picture books is a powerful way to build a young child's vocabulary.
- Picture books can help children learn to think, reason, and develop opinions.
- Picture books can help build a child's sense of place in the world and their personal identity.
- Reading picture books can help prepare a child to be successful in school.

In your hands is the guidebook my wife and I wish we had as new parents. It will teach you how to make reading come alive for your child or children with an interactive form of picture book reading that Samantha Cleaver, my coauthor, and I call "Active Reading." Active Reading is a set of research-based strategies and techniques to read books with children in a way that builds language, vocabulary, and comprehension for young children, age two through kindergarten.

This book will teach you these strategies so you can learn to shift the process of reading children's picture books from reading *to* a child to reading *with* a child. You'll learn how to become a guide to picture books, introducing your child to the characters, words, ideas, pictures, and story lines in books that you read together. The goal of Active Reading is to *have a conversation while you read the book* in a way that makes reading engaging, interactive, and fun.

To be sure, all reading is good reading. But when we engage children in Active Reading, rather than asking them to sit passively and listen to a story, we build important early reading skills and foster a love of reading. Active Reading increases the quality of the reading experience so that children look forward to reading with you and get the most out of time with books, whether it is one-on-one or with a small group of children at home or in a classroom. Active Reading with infants, toddlers, preschoolers, and elementary students is a powerful experience that will carry benefits into their later school years.

This book is a how-to guide for parents, caregivers, educators, librarians, child-care providers, and anyone else who raises, cares for, and educates a child today. We write as producers and consumers of education research; as practitioners aiding families, libraries, schools, and nonprofit providers that help children learn to read; and as parents ourselves at different points in the journey of raising proficient readers. This is your guide to getting the most out of one of the most powerful learning tools ever invented—the children's picture book—to help the child you love, care for, or educate to build critical early reading skills and develop a lifelong love of reading.

—Munro Richardson

Reading "With" versus Reading "To"

$\mathcal{I}$magine a child who loves to read. He may be curled up in an armchair with a thick novel balanced on his lap. Or she may be stretched out on a blanket in the sun, elbows dug into the ground, chin balanced on hands as her head casts a shadow on the book in front of her. Either way, they're completely absorbed in their book, until they emerge, eager to tell you all about the imaginary world they were reading about or to list off a litany of facts about bugs, planets, or animals.

Perhaps you were that child, and now favorite tattered and dog-eared titles sit on a shelf waiting for your own children to pick up. Maybe you want nothing more than to raise kids who would trade reading a good book for just about anything (and that "anything" is an ever-growing list of toys, tech, and TV). Or perhaps you were the opposite. Books, for whatever reason, didn't interest you, but you want your child to have a love of reading or at least an interest in it. Whatever your reason, raising children who love to read can seem daunting, especially when it's combined with everything else that must get done in a day with a toddler, preschooler, or kindergartener (or more than one of the above).

Compared to other activities like sports or video games, reading looks passive. There are no TV channels dedicated to watching people read. There are no long stretches of movies showing people diving into a page-turner. There are no movie montages of children sitting in a circle for story time. The most movement we see from the outside is the turning of pages and eyes scanning from line to line. But on the *inside*, children are engrossed in reading in a way that is engaging, energetic, and, well, *active*.

As adults, our minds are active when we read. Reading a novel, the story unfolds in our mind's eye. A good book seizes us from the first sentence and draws us into the world of its characters. We react to what the characters do or the choices they make (*I didn't see that coming! I can't believe he did that!*). We wonder about the implications of a story halfway in (*What will happen next? I hope the character doesn't . . .*). We have visceral reactions to the information we learn from nonfiction articles or books (*hippos' sweat turns red when they are upset!*). When we read a page-turner or interesting tidbit, we can't wait to share it with people in our lives, in conversation, through book clubs, or online.

For adult readers, these actions happen automatically, but children are still learning how to do all these things—how to understand characters and stories, how to anticipate what might happen, and how to build knowledge about the world through books. Often, children become lifelong lovers of reading by being read to by parents or other adults in their lives. As children's author Emilie Buchwald put it: "Children are made readers in the laps of their parents."

Active Reading introduces kids to a lifetime love of reading through the experience of sharing a book with an adult in their lives. It's the shift from reading "to" a child to reading "with" a child that makes Active Reading special. In typical bedtime reading, a child may curl up in a parent's lap and listen to *The Three Little Pigs* from "Once upon a time" to "happily ever after" without saying a word. Using Active Reading, the parent may ask the child to fill in the wolf's huffing and puffing and the pig's cries of "not by the hair of my chinny chin chin." The child and parent may talk about what is happening when the parent asks: What did the wolf do first? What do you think is going to happen next? They will build "background knowledge" about the durability of different building materials. They may even learn that stories can have lessons, like not to waste the day away and to work hard to keep yourself safe from danger. In Active Reading, children participate on every page.

Raising Active Readers means not just showing children that we are readers by reading on our own (we should do that too, if possible), but helping them understand how readers engage with and enjoy stories. This means talking a lot about the stories and pictures in books and asking children to share their own ideas and things they notice in the stories you read together.

Active Reading turns traditional ideas about reading to children on their head. We're not reading *to* children; we are reading *with* them. We are not asking children to sit quietly through a book. We want them to be fully engaged—with their brains, mouths, and, yes, their bodies.

Active Reading makes books come alive. Children engage with stories by pointing, talking, noticing, and exclaiming. They are animated, eager to act out *The Little Engine That Could* by Watty Piper as he climbs over the mountain or commiserate with Max as he tries to buy his favorite candy in *Bunny Cakes* by Rosemary Wells.

Active Reading makes books bigger. It invites children to talk about what they notice, see, hear, and think. They are connecting to the characters in the book by explaining how similar things have happened to them. They are listening to the story and, over time, eager to "read" the book by retelling the story page by page. These young readers are engaging in what adults love most about stories—the action, intrigue, familiarity, fun and interesting language, and connection.

When children are Active Readers, they find reading enjoyable and fun. They know that books provide entertainment and information. They are able to anticipate surprise events and revel in shocking endings. When they read on their own, understanding the story is not a struggle because they have been practicing how to think about stories for years. They become the children we imagined—hovering over a book, eyes scanning, minds engaged, completely absorbed, until they surface to tell you all about what they just read.

Active Reading is a proven way to read *with* a child rather than *to* them. The focus is on creating a conversation about the book, using the pictures and story to build a child's vocabulary and engage them in questions that get them talking about the story and how it relates to their life. Studies on Active Reading techniques (Active Reading draws from the research on dialogic reading,[1] a more formal read-aloud practice) show that children who engage with adults in Active Reading techniques have greater language skills, an important ingredient that promotes proficient reading later on.

ACTIVE READING: RAISING READERS USING DECADES OF RESEARCH

William Crain,[2] a dad in Charlotte, North Carolina, sits down with daughter Clover, age four, and the book *Room on the Broom* by Julia Donaldson.

"That witch is nice," Clover says, referring to the witch on the cover.

"Do you like Julia Donaldson?" Crain asks.

"Yeah," Clover replied. "Just like Alice Schertle."

"That's another author that you like?" Crain starts reading about the witch and her ginger hair. "Do you remember what 'ginger hair' means?"

"A bow?" Clover asks.

"It means she had red hair."

"Red hair?"

"Yeah, it means that she has red hair." Crain continues to read about a grinning cat.

"What does 'grinned' mean?"

"It means you're happy. 'Grinned' means a big smile."

"She's doing a big smile," says Clover.

"Yeah, because she's happy. They're both happy. What is the cat doing to show that he's happy?"

"Purring."

In this short introduction to a story, Crain and his daughter have talked about book authors and two words that are new for Clover. They've barely started reading the story, and already Clover is engaging with new words and the characters and connecting what she knows (that cats purr when they are happy) to the story. Crain is a parent without a teaching background who learned about Active Reading through a local library program. When he learned about Active Reading, he started changing how he read to Clover by asking more questions and spending more time talking about the words in books. For Crain, it's less about the research and more about what he sees Clover learn each time they read about the witch and the cat and the hat that was black.

Starting with a baby's first minutes, parenting seems to come with a long list of "must-dos" and "should-dos" based on any combination of grandmotherly advice, research, and magazine articles. Reading is no exception. The research on reading and what parents can do to raise readers goes back decades. In fact, the first time that Active Reading (or dialogic reading) was studied in a research setting was in the 1980s.[3]

Active Reading is a process of reading and rereading picture books that starts with the adult doing most of the reading and shifts, as the book is read over and over, to the child taking over more and more of the storytelling. The adult takes the role of a guide. They introduce the story and engage the child in conversation about the characters, ideas, places, and story in a book, providing space for the child to wonder and talk.[4]

The techniques outlined in this book, the "ABCs of Active Reading," are nothing new. They've been promoted as dialogic reading, shared reading, and interactive reading (and you may have heard others). The term "Active Reading" refers to the collection of read-aloud approaches and practices, including dialogic reading, shared reading, interactive reading, and others. Here is an overview of research findings on Active Reading practices.

Active Reading is an excellent activity to build kids' language and early reading skills. As a teaching practice, Active Reading is an evidence-based practice, meaning that it has a strong research base to support its use in the classroom.[5] Over the past thirty years, education researchers have studied what happens when adults engage groups of children in books using Active Reading techniques compared to similar groups of children who listen passively as books are read to them. Taken together, the studies have established Active Reading as an "activity par excellence" that builds children's oral language and ability to understand and recognize letter sounds.

In other words, Active Reading is one of the most impactful strategies to build children's early language and vocabulary skills that can be done at home, in child-care programs, and in early education classrooms.

Active Reading works with many children from different places, backgrounds, and experiences. Active Reading is not just for kids who need extra help, though it is effective for children who may need extra support.[6] These techniques have been proven to work with children from low-income and higher-income homes[7] and those who speak both English and other languages.[8]

Active Reading works in home and at school. When preschool teachers used Active Reading techniques (asking open-ended questions, responding to children using Talk More, and building vocabulary, among others), children used more words when talking (i.e., "expressive language").[9] In one study on Active Reading done in the home, parents were told to do Active Reading with their child at home every day for four weeks and were provided with some support from researchers. Children whose parents used Active Reading techniques had greater vocabulary and improved early reading and writing skills compared to children who were not engaged in Active Reading.[10]

Active Reading is better when done both at home and school. Researchers have studied what happens when children experience Active Reading both at school and home, and children whose teachers and parents both engaged in Active Reading had the greatest gains.[11] In one study, children were engaged in Active Reading at their school for ten minutes each day, then some children were also provided with books to read at home and parents were told to read every day. Parents reported reading to their children between eight and fifty-three times in that six weeks (which makes us think that these parents had as busy schedules as the rest of us and may not have gotten to read to their child every day).

Still, children who were read to both at home and at school had higher scores than those who were just read to at school or who did not experience Active Reading at all.[12] For us, this means that it's important for children to receive Active Reading at home and school, if they attend school, and that parents don't have to be perfect. Doing some Active Reading is better than none.

Active Reading can have long-lasting impacts. Active Reading focuses on building kids' language—their ability to understand what they hear and their ability to use lots of words when they talk. Language is the foundation that children use to understand what they read when they are in elementary school and beyond. Active Reading builds a strong foundation in the language skills that kids use throughout their lives. For example, when preschool teachers used

Active Reading techniques (such as explaining why characters act in certain ways), children had higher vocabulary skills in kindergarten and fourth grade.[13]

Active Reading impacts many child reading outcomes. Children need to have many skills in order to read on their own (more on this in chapter 2), and Active Reading has shown to develop these skills, including oral language and vocabulary, as well as alphabet knowledge (their ability to identify the letters in the alphabet), print awareness (knowing how words work in a book),[14] and phonemic awareness (understanding of the sounds in words).[15]

What to Remember

• There are two parts of language ability: the words children can say (expressive language) and the words they can understand (receptive language).
• Children's language ability at age three begins to predict how well they will read in third grade.
• Active Reading is a proven way to help build children's oral language and vocabulary, important skills that will help them to become proficient readers. Active Reading also supports other early reading skills, including alphabet knowledge, print awareness, and phonemic awareness.
• Active Reading techniques have decades of research to support them and are effective when parents and teachers incorporate them at school and home. Active Reading can be done a few times a week and still produce benefits for kids.

THE ABCS OF ACTIVE READING

Active Reading means engaging a child in three things while reading: **A**sking questions, **B**uilding vocabulary, and **C**onnecting with the child's world. Together these are the "ABCs" of Active Reading. There is no set number of times you have to read a book and no prescribed way to read it. You don't even have to finish the book to have done Active Reading well; the focus is on having a conversation about the story, the words in the book, and the connections that you can make.

The best way to do Active Reading is to *experience a picture book* with a child, or small group of children, and try to find something new to talk about each time. As an adult, your job is to be a guide to the book, helping the child to learn and engage with the characters, words, and ideas in the story and letting them take the lead.

Future chapters will delve deeper into the ABCs. This section provides an overview of the aspects that make Active Reading so effective: joint attention, the Talk More prompt, fill-in-the-blank prompts, Asking questions, Building vocabulary, and Connecting to the child's world.

Joint Attention

Joint attention is when the adult and the child are focusing on the same thing in the book. It involves helping your child see what you're looking at in the story or talking about what your child is interested in. When Crain and his daughter spent time looking at the picture of the purring cat and the grinning witch at the start of *Room on the Broom*, he was implementing joint attention. This simple act of following what the child is interested in, pointing at pictures in books, and talking about what you're both looking at increases the number of words children learn.[16] (Joint attention is covered in chapter 2.)

Talk More

The goal of Active Reading is to have a conversation, and the Talk More sequence shows children how to use language correctly, gives them more language about the topic they are talking about, and encourages them to expand their thinking.[17] (Talk More is covered more completely in chapter 3.)

For example, Monica McMahon, a mom in Charlotte, North Carolina, and her then two-year-old son, Jude, sat down with a book, *Turtle and Snake go Camping* by Kate Spohn. They look at a picture of Turtle, Snake, and a pile of things for their camping trip. McMahon reads about the first-aid kit and asks Jude, "Do you know what a first-aid kit is?"

Jude shakes his head no.

"It's a kit or small package of items that helps if someone gets hurt. What might be in your first-aid kit?"

"Like a Band-Aid?" asks Jude.

"A Band-Aid, that's right," replies McMahon. "That's a good guess and that's right. A first-aid kit is a package of things that has a Band-Aid in them. There's other stuff too, but this red symbol right there," she points to a red cross on the first-aid box in the picture, "that shows a first-aid kit."

In this exchange, McMahon asked a question using the picture for reference and, between McMahon's repetition of Jude's responses and asking additional prompts, they talked about what could be in a first-aid kit. That's the essence of Talk More: taking what the child says (or points at) and building it into a conversation.

Talk More is also one of the main ways that Active Reading changes over time. The way that two-year-old Jude engages with a book will be much different than how four-year-old Jude will. A two-year-old uses brief sentences, compared to a four- or five-year-old who is able to use much longer and complex responses and can connect what is read to other stories and their own experiences. But, whatever the age of the child, the goal of Talk More is the same, to lengthen and expand what the child says.

Fill-in-the-Blank

Fill-in-the-blank or completion prompts[18] occur when adults leave off parts of the text for children to fill in. When reading *Little Blue Truck*, the child may fill in the sounds the animal makes or the truck's "Beep! Beep! Beep!" This increases their expressive and receptive language.[19] (Fill-in-the-blank is covered in chapter 2.)

Asking Questions

We ask questions to build children's knowledge and to draw attention to details in the story.[20] There are two types of questions that are the focus of Active Reading: story questions and open-ended questions. Story questions ask about the story itself. For example, when reading *Bunny Cakes* by Rosemary Wells, story questions you could ask are:

- What is Max doing?
- What does Ruby want to do?
- What happens to the eggs?
- What does Max want?

Each of these questions asks children to pay attention to details in the story and follow the plot, or series of events.

Story questions are important, but they may be "closed" or have only one answer. Open-ended questions provide opportunity for more conversation about the story. These include questions that ask children to infer information, make predictions, and form opinions. Unlike story questions, the answers to these questions may change as children grow and develop knowledge and experiences. Reading *Bunny Cakes*, you may ask:

- What else could Ruby have done?
- How could Max have told the grocery what he wanted?
- Why was Grandma thrilled about the cakes?
- How else might she have felt?

Open-ended questions combined with strong language modeling are an important tool; children in pre-kindergarten can be taught to infer and predict.[21] (Asking questions is covered more in chapter 4.)

Build Vocabulary

A child's vocabulary is an important predictor of later reading achievement.[22] Specifically, vocabulary supports reading comprehension by helping children make inferences when they read words and phrases.[23] Picture books offer exposure to language that is not commonly included in conversational language,[24] and vocabulary questions teach children new words by helping them define the words and use the words.

For example, the book *An Orange in January* by Dianna Hutts Aston, the story of how an orange goes from tree to grocery store to being shared with friends, provides an opportunity to define and talk about the words *feasted*, *soil*, *breath*, and *drenched*. (Building vocabulary is covered in chapter 5.)

Connect to the Child's World

Connecting to the child's world involves building language through interactions that ask the child to make explicit connections to experiences as well as to other stories they have read.[25] This helps children understand the context for stories and builds background knowledge that supports later reading comprehension.[26] While reading *An Orange in January*, a child may connect with the experience of picking fruit or of sharing a special food with friends. (Connecting to the child's world is covered more in chapter 6.)

What to Remember

- In Active Reading, your job is to be a guide to the book, introducing the child to the characters, words, and ideas in the story.
- Focusing on the same things in the book (joint attention), encouraging conversation about the book (Talk More), and letting your child fill in some of the words (fill-in-the-blank) are three key strategies that you use to engage your child in the book.
- Active Reading involves Asking questions, Building vocabulary, and Connecting to the child's world while you read.
- There is no set number of times you have to read a book and no particular way you have to read it. You don't even have to finish a book to do Active Reading well.

WHEN TO DO ACTIVE READING:
TAKING ADVANTAGE OF CHILD DEVELOPMENT

Like many parents, I remember my daughter Saha's first word (*dada*), and for the next few months, I knew her entire vocabulary. I could list off the words she knew (*no, more, baby, banana*). But, at some point in her toddler years, I couldn't remember exactly which words she did and didn't know. Then she started surprising me by telling me that something was *annoying* or that bears *hibernate*. Her vocabulary had quickly outgrown the running list of words that I kept in my head.

Around age one, children say their first word: *mama, dada,* "baba" for bottle, or "bub" for bubble. For a few months, they add words quickly—two to three per week—to their vocabularies as they learn to name objects in their world and request items they want.[27]

Starting in toddlerhood, children learn words quickly and learn how to use language (changing "you" to "I" when they respond to a question, for example).[28] This period of language growth extends into early elementary school. All this language learning sets the stage for reading. Children with larger vocabularies generally find it easier to learn how to read. It's a lot easier when a child is learning to sound out words they already know. *This is why Active Reading is so important for kids who are ages two to five—it's during this period that kids are doing a lot of language learning.* Of course, in order to build extensive vocabularies, we have to teach kids new words and engage them in talking about words.

Reading to children, it's easy to see how children develop the ability to understand language ("receptive language"). They're hearing lots of language each time you read to them. For example, one way that reading books helps kids learn words is by exposing them to words in multiple books.[29] The word "soil" is used both in *Some Smug Slug* by Pamela Edwards and in *An Orange in January*. But language learning is not a passive activity; it's an active process. Reading with children provides the opportunity for children to have lots of language modeled for them (when we talk about what we see on a page) and to practice language themselves (when we ask them to answer questions or describe what they see happening on a page).

📖

What to Remember

• When children are between the ages of two and five, they are learning words and language at a fast rate. This is an ideal time to do Active Reading.

- Children must be engaged in both listening to language and using language; that's why reading lots of books and talking about the words that you find in books is so important.

LEARNING TO LOVE BOOKS

Thinking back to the child who loves reading, they're a bookworm because they can read well, understand what they read, and enjoy reading. So far, Active Reading, with all the types of questions to remember and the focus on outcomes, may feel academic. While there are clear benefits for kids' language and reading, it should also be fun.

Active Reading should incorporate lots of hugs, encouragement, praise, and high-fives. For kids, simply having the one-on-one attention and the opportunity to talk to you will be rewarding enough to make reading books a fun activity. Also, during Active Reading, we want children to feel successful when they read with you because they answered a question, told you the meaning of a word, or filled in a word from the story. If Active Reading ever isn't fun, or if the child you're reading with is bored or resistant, stop reading and do something they are interested in!

When kids are read to at home, the results are evident as they start school. Kindergarten teachers gave higher marks in oral language to children who grew up listening to more stories between the ages of one and three compared to their classmates who heard fewer stories during the same time period.[30] Preparing kids for a life of reading is about more than just reading stories. Reading *with* children helps kids' language and literacy skills grow faster than when they are read *to*. In fact, it's the quality of book reading experiences (more than other factors, including family income level) that a child has in preschool that is related to the size of their vocabulary later in life.[31]

The goal of this book is to give you the knowledge and skills to make reading time—whether it's one-on-one with your own child or with a few children that you teach—a fun experience now and a powerful experience that will carry benefits into their school years. Throughout this book, we will explain and explore the components of Active Reading with examples from actual parents. In the next chapter, we will discuss how children learn to read and how joint attention and learning about how books and print work can help children's early reading skills.

• 2 •

Learning to Read

Joint Attention, Print Concepts, and Print Knowledge

"*W*here is Papa going with that ax?" In the opening scene of *Charlotte's Web* by E. B. White, Fern sees her father leaving the kitchen for the hog house with an ax in hand. She is horrified to learn that her father is going to kill a runt piglet that was born the previous night and runs out to save it. In the first pages of this classic children's novel, readers must form a picture of the scene in their mind, from Fern and her mother talking in the kitchen to Fern's pleas with her father in the hog house. In their introduction to the character of Fern, they start to understand Fern as a compassionate character, and what it means to save a runt pig—that he is a pig that will need extra attention.

By the fourth grade, children should be able to read and enjoy *Charlotte's Web*. A lot happens in a child's early years to help a child become a reader who can read words, understand individual words and sentences, and follow a story from scene to scene. The work that young children do as they learn language helps them become readers that can understand what's happening in stories and novels, enjoy literature, and fall in love with characters like Wilbur the pig and Charlotte the spider that have enthralled children for generations.

On the first day of kindergarten, children arrive at school with skills and knowledge that they will use to learn to read. These skills develop long before entering the classroom. Kids who start pre-kindergarten and kindergarten with some pre-reading skills (or the skills that come before those we need to read well) are poised to become stronger readers than those who do not.[1] The good news is that virtually all children can develop the ability to read. Doing Active Reading with a young child builds those skills that they need to be "on track" to read well by the time they sit for that first-day-of-school photo. In this chapter, we will cover how children learn to read and how those core skills are helpful for children when they arrive at kindergarten, starting with how school-aged children progress from learning to read to reading to learn.

LEARNING TO READ VERSUS READING TO LEARN

The work of children in kindergarten and first and second grades is learning to read. In these grades, children learn letter sounds (that *s* says "s" like in "sun"), letter patterns (that *igh* says "I" as in the word "light"), and how to read longer words and sentences. In school, children spend time sounding out words and reading simple sentences so that they can read many different types of words quickly.

In general, the information that children learn is presented by the teacher. Any information that children must learn, if it is in a book, will be read aloud to them. For example, in a lesson about the life cycle of a butterfly, children listen to a book about butterflies, look at pictures of the four stages, put them in order, and then watch a video about how caterpillars become butterflies. They aren't expected to read all that information on their own.

In third grade, how children learn new information changes. Now they are expected to use their reading skills to read and understand new information. So in science and social studies, while children will still engage with information through experiments, demonstrations, and videos, they will increasingly be asked to read a book to get new information. A child may be given a novel and asked to read a chapter before coming to talk about what he read, or the class may read a short passage about the water cycle before discussing what they learned. So while reading is not the only way that children will learn information (and this is true for adults as well), being able to learn new information by reading is a skill that becomes increasingly important.

Also in upper elementary school (grades 3 through 5), less time is spent teaching students how to read. This means that children who do not have strong reading skills by the end of third grade often fall behind and rarely catch up.[2] In fact, children who read well in third grade are more likely to graduate high school on time and succeed in college and their careers.[3]

On the other hand, children who are not reading well in third grade are more likely to struggle through school, drop out of high school, and struggle with later career success.[4] It is a great concern that in 2015, 64 percent of fourth graders in the United States did not read proficiently.[5] The percent of fourth graders who are not reading proficiently is significantly higher for low-income (78 percent), black (81 percent), Hispanic (78 percent), and non-native-English-speaking (92 percent) students.[6] (Visit the Campaign for Grade Level Reading at www.gradelevelreading.net for more information.) Children aren't expected to read to learn until upper elementary school, but early reading experiences impact *how well* they are able to make the leap from listening to learn to reading to learn.

What to Remember

- When children are in kindergarten through second grade, they spend a great deal of time during their school day learning to read.
- Third grade is a turning point in a child's education, when they are expected to apply their reading skills to learn new information from what they read.
- When children have proficient reading skills by third grade, they are more likely to succeed in school and in life.
- Early reading experiences provide children with the foundation they need to read proficiently in third grade.

HOW CHILDREN LEARN TO READ

When children sit down to read a book on their own, they bring their knowledge of letters and sounds together with their understanding of word meanings (vocabulary), their understanding of how language works (the rules of grammar and how sentences are put together), and their knowledge about the world. Then they must do this throughout an entire sentence, story, or book. It's no easy task!

There are five core reading skills that children need to be strong readers: phonemic awareness, phonics, fluency, vocabulary, and comprehension.[7]

1. Phonemic Awareness

A parent sings the familiar Raffi song "Down by the Bay" with her two-year-old in the car. A teacher asks children to say all the words that rhyme with *dog* that they can think of. The children shout out: *log, pollywog, hog, bog.* Both of these activities build children's phonemic awareness, or the ability to hear, separate, and manipulate or change sounds in words.

Language is made up of phonemes, or the smallest segments of sounds. For example, the word "whale" has five letters, but only three sounds /wh/ /long a/ and /l/. The word "melt" has four sounds, one for each letter: /m/ /e/ /l/ /t/. A child's phonemic awareness is one of the strongest contributors to their reading success.[8]

Teaching phonemic awareness involves listening to words, identifying similarities and differences in words (like words that rhyme or do not rhyme), identifying the individual sounds in words, and combining sounds into words. While phonemic awareness can be taught, it is also naturally developed through many activities that young children already enjoy, like reciting nursery rhymes, singing rhyming songs, and reading rhyming books like Dr. Seuss's *The Cat in the Hat*. Children develop phonemic awareness starting in toddlerhood and continue through first grade, when most children have developed strong phonemic awareness skills. (Chapter 7 covers how to build phonemic awareness through Active Reading.)

2. Phonics

Phonics is what we think of when we think about learning to read words. When children learn phonics, they learn that letters and combinations of letters represent sounds that come together to make words. For example, when children learn the sounds that the letters *b*, *a*, and *n* make, they can sound out the words "an," "ban," and "nab." When a child learns that when an *e* is added to the end of the word, the vowel in the middle changes from a short to a long vowel sound, they can read the words "shin" and "shine," or "tap" and "tape." Children learn phonics during their first years of schooling.

3. Fluency

Fluency is the speed, accuracy (number of words read correct), and expression that we have when reading. Fluent reading, when text is read easily and with expression, is enjoyable to listen to—think about how an audiobook sounds. When children struggle to read one word at a time, they are not able to gain a broader understanding of the sentences and paragraphs they are reading. And when they do not read punctuation, like excitement into exclamation points, and they are not able to add appropriate expression to what they are reading, they also lose important meaning.

It is important to note that children can read too fast. When children read too quickly, they are not able to grasp meaning from what they read. So, rather than thinking about reading quickly, we think about reading at a pace that allows children to understand what they are reading. If a child read words on a page correctly but cannot tell you what he read about, it may be because he read either too slow or too fast.

Children will start to practice fluency at the end of first grade and will continue to practice through elementary school. As a parent, you can expose your child to fluent reading during Active Reading when you read with expression, including adding silly voices to characters or reading with a dramatic voice.

4. Vocabulary

A child's vocabulary consists of the words that he knows, understands, and uses. A child may have a basic understanding of a word (that an engine is something that makes a vehicle go) or a deep understanding (that there are many different types of engines and that an engine can also refer to what makes something happen outside of a vehicle, as an "engine of change"). When children have strong vocabularies, they are more likely to understand what they read.[9]

Children start developing their vocabulary at birth and continue through their lifetimes. In fact, vocabulary is one of the most important aspects of reading that we can influence in young children who are already learning words very quickly. (In chapter 5, we discuss how to build vocabulary through Active Reading).

5. Comprehension

Comprehension, understanding what is read, is the goal of reading. Comprehension involves understanding the meaning of words on the page, how those words come together to create meaning, and what information an author has included in a text that we can use to make inferences. Thus, comprehension involves literally understanding the words and sentences, reading "between the lines" to make inferences, and reading beyond the lines to draw connections to bigger ideas and concepts. Children understand what they read when they combine their background knowledge, or what they know about the world, with information from the text.

For example, in the book *Where the Wild Things Are* by Maurice Sendak, a little boy, Max, is sent to his room without supper. Looking at the image on the page, you can see Max glaring at the closed door with his arms over his chest. From this information, and from their knowledge that time-out is not a pleasant experience, children can infer that Max is upset. It would be incorrect to say that Max is happy at this point in the story.

Two specific skills that build comprehension are kids' receptive vocabulary (how well they understand spoken words) and narrative comprehension, or their understanding of how a story progresses.[10] Children develop comprehension alongside reading skill, and the stronger their foundation in language and vocabulary, the easier it is for children to eventually understand what they read.

It's obvious that children have a lot of learning to do to become strong readers. Active Reading targets some of those early reading skills, mostly vocabulary and comprehension, through the development of language and vocabulary. It can also target phonemic awareness when we engage kids in thinking about words in books. It does not address phonics and fluency directly, as those are skills that young children either have not reached yet (fluency) or that are best taught using explicit instruction, like the teaching that they will receive in school (phonics).

Skills Children Need to Read

Reading Skill	*What It Is*	*When Children Develop This Skill*	*A Good Way to Teach It*
Phonemic Awareness	The ability to hear the individual sounds in words, put sounds together to form words, or change words by changing one sound to another (*ball* to *wall*). This is an auditory skill; children do not need to read print to be good at this skill.	Preschool into first grade	Playing with words (rhyming games and songs) and practice
Phonics	The ability to identify letters and their sounds and read letter sounds and patterns in words. Children read letters on the page and apply their knowledge of sounds to read words.	Kindergarten into second grade	Explicit instruction in school
Fluency	The ability to read words, sentences, and paragraphs accurately and at a pace that helps you understand what you read.	First grade into upper elementary school	Practice with lots of different texts and feedback from a teacher
Vocabulary	The knowledge of words, what they mean, and how to use them.	Birth through school	Active Reading and talking about the words that your child hears each day
Comprehension	Understanding what you read, including what is written on the page (literal meaning) and what you can infer from the information the author provides.	Birth through school	Active Reading and engaging your child in lots of language

What to Remember

- There are five skills that students must master to become proficient readers: phonemic awareness, phonics, fluency, vocabulary, and comprehension.
- Phonemic awareness is the ability to manipulate the sounds in words.
- Phonics is an understanding of how written letters translate into spoken language.
- Fluency is the ability to read words with appropriate accuracy, rate, and expression.
- Vocabulary is a child's knowledge of words, including the number of words they know and how well they understand each word.
- Comprehension is the ability to understand what is read, including skills like making inferences.
- Active Reading targets children's vocabulary and comprehension and can build phonemic awareness.

LEARNING TO READ: THE EARLY YEARS

For both my daughters, their first reading experience was days after they were born. Sitting on the couch at home, propped delicately in my lap, I read each of them their first board books, Sandra Boynton's *But Not the Hippopotamus*, Karen Katz's *Counting Kisses*, Bill Martin's *Brown Bear, Brown Bear*. The point was not for them to understand every word but to start the habit of reading as close to their birth days as possible.

Even for babies, learning to read starts with these first experiences. This is why reading to your baby is on every parenting to-do list. Consider what just one book can teach a child: The book *Freight Train* by Donald Crews is a classic board book about a train with different colored cars. *Freight Train* teaches children not only colors but about words related to trains (*track, caboose, tank car, hopper car, steam engine*) and movement and travel (*tunnel, cities, trestles*) and about present and past tense (*going, going, gone*). All that in a book that takes seconds to read and has a total of fifty-five words on twelve sturdy pages.

Learning Language to Learn to Read

Children need strong language skills to learn to read well, both the ability to understand what is said to them and the ability to communicate their own ideas. It might sound strange that we need to teach children language, since they seem to pick it up without any instruction at all. A child toddles up to you and demands, "Juice." A two-year-old points to the cat in a book and says, "Meow, cat." But even these early interactions have lots of language learning behind them.

We talk, kids listen, and word by word they start to communicate. The two-year-old asks for "more orange juice please." The three-year-old identifies a "cat napping on the porch because he is tired" in the same book he identified only the "meow, cat" before. It might not seem like it from the text in some early books (*Brown bear, brown bear, what do you see?* is not the most complex of sentences), but all books reinforce more complex language rules than spoken language.

The Language of Storybooks

One of the reasons that storybooks are so important is that they expose kids to language that they don't hear all day, every day.[11] Think back over your day. What do you say to your kids the most? If you have a three-year-old (as I do at the writing of this book), it may be sentences like: *What do you want? Eat your breakfast. Put your shoes on. Shoes on. Shoes!* At home and in classrooms, a lot of daily language—including best practices like narrating daily routines ("Now I'm making your lunch; I am going to put the peas and pasta on the plate")—focuses on what's happening in the child's world in the moment. This type of talk—prompting children to follow directions, talking about what you are doing as you follow a recipe to make muffins—is important. These conversations take children through situations that are related to their immediate experience.

While reading with four-year-old Clover, William Crain opens the book *The Sniffles for Bear* by Bonnie Becker and starts to read, describing the sick bear's throat as sore and gruffly.

"What's 'gruffly'?" four-year-old Clover asks.

"It's like sore," replies Blaine, "but you remember how you sounded when you were sick?"

"Yeah."

"I think that's what they're saying with gruffly. They're saying like gravelly," Crain says in a gravelly voice. He continues reading.

We also want kids to hear lots of language that takes them beyond their immediate experience, like when Clover had to think back to a time when she was sick and relate it to Bear's experience. Picture books help children understand how language can be situated in the future, the past, or another time altogether. Their ability to understand and talk about the abstract concepts that they hear about in books is very important.

Another benefit of talking about storybooks is the length and complexity of language used. In everyday conversation, our sentences are short, we use the same words over and over, and we tend to rely on gestures and other nonverbal motions.[12] In contrast, picture books often have longer, more complex sentences, like Mouse's announcement in *The Sniffles for Bear* and the description of Mouse, that add complexity to the language that children are exposed to.

What about Active Reading When Kids Can Already Read?

Children enjoy being read to long past the point that they can read on their own, but it may feel a bit silly to read a picture book with a young child who can read the words independently. Active Reading is still important for preschool and kindergarten-age children who know how to read (or decode) words. Reading words on the page (phonics and fluency) are aspects of reading that are not taught through Active Reading. Even when children can read a word, they may not know what it means. That's where Active Reading comes in and supports the skills that will help them make meaning when they sound out words on their own.

What to Remember

- Storybooks are important for young children because they provide access to formal, written language, as well as more complex language and language that is outside of the child's immediate experience.
- Active Reading is important for children who are able to read words in part for the shared experience of reading and also for the conversation about the story.

SHARING A STORY: JOINT ATTENTION

Reading a book with a young child requires your attention, and your child's, but not in the way that you might think. When I started putting Active Reading into practice at my house, I started looking at my daughter's face when we read. I wanted to see where she was looking on the page. Then I pointed at what she was looking at and talked about that, rather than talking about what I noticed on the page.

The attention that is required to do Active Reading is about more than reading the words on the page. It involves noticing how your child engages with the pictures, characters, words, and ideas in the book either by listening to their responses or reading their nonverbal cues (pointing, looking). When adults are highly responsive and child-oriented, they are focused on what the child is interested in, asking questions and encouraging the child to respond and engage in conversation.[13] For adults, this means creating opportunities to focus on the same thing for a period of time. It's as simple as asking the child what they see, leaving a few seconds for the child to look at the pictures and respond, and then talking about that. It seems obvious and easy, but it can have a powerful influence on what children learn when you read together.[14]

One of the reasons joint attention is so effective is that it provides children with specific, individualized encouragement and support that increase children's word knowledge and acquisition.[15] Reading with one child, you may look to see where your child is focused on the page and ask him to talk about that picture. Or, with a few children, you may look to see what has interested one child and encourage all the children to notice the same aspect of the picture. For example, while reading *Flower Garden* by Eve Bunting, one child may be very interested in the types of flowers that the girl is buying, while another wants to talk about what is in the shopping cart. Asking each child what she sees creates a conversation about the picture that draws on both children's attention.

Being aware of joint attention also stops us adults from some bad habits that we may have while reading—namely, going too fast. Adults, because we understand the book (and may have read it many times before), may ask a question and move on without leaving enough time for the child to think of an answer.[16] Sometimes we may be pressed for time and just want to get through the book. We may just turn the pages too quickly, not giving the child enough time to look at what they are interested in. Knowing that joint attention is important may help you slow down and wait before moving on with the story. Remember, you don't have to finish the book to do Active Reading well!

Another aspect of joint attention is pointing. This is as simple as it sounds: pointing at pictures that you are naming or pointing to the illustration you are referring to when you read or talk about the book. Young children need to know exactly what we adults are talking about when we talk about the cow in the barn in *Big Red Barn* by Margaret Wise Brown or the escalator in *Corduroy* by Don Freeman. Pointing to pictures in stories helps children connect words we say with pictures in books, and eventually the objects in their worlds.

Over time, practicing joint attention while reading creates a positive, encouraging environment during reading that gives kids space to learn and sets the stage for a love of reading. This is important: *when adults are warm and encouraging, children learn more language and literacy skills and are more eager to read.*[17]

📖
What to Remember

• Joint attention occurs when the child or children and the adult are focused on the same aspect of a book, the pictures, or the text.

• Joint attention encourages conversation about the story and helps adults slow down and provide the child with time to respond.

• Simply providing joint attention improves kids' language and fosters a love of reading.

• As part of joint attention, pointing at pictures in the book to show your child what you are referring to can help them learn new vocabulary.

TEACHING THE BASICS OF BOOKS

Reading *The Sniffles for Bear*, Crain reads the title and author, Bonnie Becker. "And who wrote the outside?" asks Clover. "Who drew the pictures? Who drew this one on the outside?"

"The illustrator drew all the pictures, even the one on the cover," Crain explains.

"And who did this plastic?"

"Well, that's special library binding. It helps keep the book safe when lots of children are using it."

"And the illustrator drew all of these?"

"Yes, and Bonnie Becker, the author, wrote all the words."

"All the outside words?"

"She wrote *all* the words in the book."

Through this conversation, Crain is teaching Clover how to understand important aspects of a book—the author and illustrator—and the roles of those two people. He's also responding to Clover's curiosity about how books are similar: Do all authors write the title of their books? Does the illustrator draw the picture on the cover of the book, too?

In addition to hearing lots of language, children can learn early rules about reading books, such as the front and back cover, spine, author, and illustrator.[18] (Adults often take these rules for granted.) When reading the text, teaching children about books and written words (print knowledge) teaches them important skills that they will apply to every reading session. In fact, phonemic awareness and print knowledge explain the majority of the difference in how well children read in first grade.[19] Active Reading is an effective way to teach children these core concepts before they start kindergarten, giving them a head start when it comes to learning how to read books on their own.

Print Concepts

A child who has strong print concepts knows how to use a book. She knows how to hold a book, how to turn the pages, and how to start looking at images and words (from left to right). The print concepts that children must learn can be different depending on culture (for example, Asian cultures may read from top to bottom and right to left.) Children must be taught how to operate a book in the appropriate way for their culture. Teaching print concepts directly, or naming the aspects of book knowledge and ensuring that children know how to find each on new books, is an efficient way to teach your child these concepts.

Talking about the parts of a book does more than teach your child how to find the author and illustrator; it is related to comprehension. Remember, comprehension involves literally understanding the words on the line, reading between the lines to make inferences, and reading beyond the lines to draw connections to bigger ideas and concepts. Children who are strong readers understand that the title gives meaning that they can use to understand what they are about to read, and they use the title to anticipate what will happen in the rest of the text.[20] Strong readers also understand basics of how a book works, for example, that there is a beginning and ending.[21] You can teach print concepts during Active Reading:

• First, point to the title, author, and illustrator *before* you read. Then ask your child to point to the title, author, and illustrator.

• Ask, "What do you think the book will be about?" Use the cover illustration to talk about the story and what may happen. For example, there is the picture of a girl and flowers on the cover of *Flower Garden* by Eve Bunting. You may ask, "What do you think we'll see in this book?" Then talk about the girl as a character, the flowers you see, and what the word "garden" means.

• If your child likes a book by a particular author or illustrator, find more books by that author and talk about how all these books are written or drawn by the same person.

• Encourage your child to use the titles of books when he asks to read. Ask, "What is the title of the book you want us to read?"

Print Knowledge

When Saha (age three) and I started reading *Where the Wild Things Are*, I asked her to point to where we start reading. Saha points to the picture of Max making mischief.

"No, the picture shows us the story," I correct; "the words tell the story."

"Oh." Saha points to the words on the page.

"That's right," I say. "What letters do you see in that first word?"

"T, H, E," says Saha, pointing to each letter.

"Right! That word is 'the.'"

"The," Saha repeats.

Later, when we get to the page where Max sails off in a private boat. Saha points to the letters on the side of Max's boat. "Those letters are M, A, X," she says. "That's his name."

"That's right. M, A, X says Max."

Print knowledge is a child's understanding of how written words have meaning.[22] A child with strong print knowledge will be able to point to where to start reading on a page and knows that the words, not the pictures, tell the story. She knows that words are made up of letters and that there are spaces between words. She may also count the number of words in a sentence or letters in a word. These skills are some of those identified as particularly important as children enter school, as children who have these skills do better with early reading than children who do not.[23]

How much children learn about print during Active Reading depends on how often adults stop to talk about and explain the rules of printed text.[24] While all reading with children is good reading, Active Reading helps us intentionally use books to help children develop print knowledge. Children must be involved in talking about the print in books and how it impacts the story in order for them to learn about print from Active Reading. Some ways to teach print knowledge during Active Reading:

• Read the same book over and over again. This provides an opportunity to talk about the different ways text is used in a story. Once the child is familiar with the story, they may be more interested in talking about how the words are laid out on the page, where we start reading, and where each sentence ends.[25]

• Read stories that emphasize letters and words, such as *I Stink* by Kate McMullan, which uses different fonts in the illustrations and text, or books that use alliteration or rhyme like *Some Smug Slug* by Pamela Edwards.

• Point to the words as you read them, and show your child how you drop to the next line and continue reading when you get to the end of a line. Ask your child to follow along with his finger as you read so he learns that words are read from left to right and top to bottom.

• Ask your child to point to the place where you start reading on a few pages each time you read.

• Help your child learn upper- and lowercase letters by pointing to letters and naming them or asking your child to find letters on the page. Start with the letters in your child's name and build from there. Reading alphabet books provides lots of ways to talk about letters. (There is a list of good alphabet books in appendix A.)

• Point to and name punctuation. Talk about what each type of punctuation means (a question mark means that we are asking a question, an exclamation point means that something is exciting).

• Teach your child how to read punctuation by modeling reading fluency. Exaggerate how you read certain punctuation marks (read a sentence with an exclamation point with extra energy).

• Help your child understand that words are separated by spaces. Show your child how to count the number of words in a title or in short sentences on a page. Then have your child practice too.

You can also teach your child print knowledge outside of Active Reading:

• Encourage your child to "write" letters, lists, and birthday cards.

• Create word labels for objects in your house (bed, refrigerator, chair).

• Point out letters in your everyday surroundings, like the signs in the grocery store, the letters on a stop sign, or names on buildings.

What to Remember

• Print concepts, or how to use a book, can be taught early and supports children's comprehension and understanding of how stories work.

• Print knowledge is a child's understanding of how words written on the page hold meaning and how to read them and can be taught by incorporating pointing out and teaching print knowledge during Active Reading.

LEARNING TO READ

Reading aloud accomplishes many things—it's fun, helps kids wind down before bedtime, and teaches them new words. But how we read books with children can teach our children different knowledge and skills. Focusing on the story while reading teaches kids to understand language. Focusing on words and letters in books is related to kids' learning important preliteracy skills. In chapter 3, we will discuss how to start engaging children in conversations about books through picture walks and Talk More.

• 3 •

How to Read a Book

Repeated Reading, Fill-in-the-Blank,
Picture Walks, and Talk More

Neina, my two-year-old daughter, brings me the book *Flower Garden* by Eve Bunting. "Will you read it to me?" she asks.

"Sure," I take the book, scoop her up into my lap, and open to the first page. "This is a new book; it's called *Flower Garden*. What do you see on this page?" I ask.

"A girl," says Neina.

"That's right; here is a girl," I say, pointing. "What is the girl doing?"

"She's riding the cart," says Neina.

"She is riding on a grocery cart. What else do you see?"

"Flowers."

"There are flowers in the cart. What color flowers do you see?"

Neina points to red, yellow, and purple flowers.

$\mathscr{A}$ picture walk involves talking about the pictures, naming objects, and even starting to tell the story before reading a word in a picture book. This practice, and the conversation that follows, gives Neina an opportunity to learn new words and develop her language. Talking about pictures makes use of what children already do best—finding details in illustrations—to start a conversation about the book. As a parent, talking about the illustrations before reading the book gives kids a chance to show what they already know. A picture walk is also a way to build kids' language page by page.

In chapter 2, we discussed the importance of language as the foundation for reading and how Active Reading is a way to build your child's language skills. This chapter builds on that with information about how children progress in language learning and about Active Reading practices that support kids' language, including repeated reading, fill-in-the-blank prompts, picture walks, and Talk More.

EARLY LANGUAGE AND ACTIVE READING

Babies enter the world primed and ready to learn language. By their second birthday, children can identify the sounds of their native language; ask for objects, people, and activities; and even put multiple words together in basic sentences. By the time they say their first word, children understand that language is a powerful tool that they can use to get what they want, whether that's a bottle of milk or Mom's attention.

As children learn language, they must learn the names for all the things in their world, including objects, people, ideas, and other concepts (think: holidays, days of the week). They must learn how to ask and answer questions: *What are you playing with? I'm playing with a doll.* They must learn how to refer to themselves and things that are theirs: *I want my toy.* And they'll think about things that happen in the future or the past: *I went to the park. We are going to the zoo.* All this happens by the time they are three.

Active Reading uses books as a jumping-off point to build kids' language. The goal of Active Reading is that the child takes over more and more of the talking during reading sessions so that the child progresses from naming things in the book to telling portions of the story themselves.

📖
What to Remember

• By the time a child is three, he will likely be able to speak in full sentences, ask and answer questions, and use language for a variety of purposes.
• Active Reading develops kids' language by encouraging them to take over more and more of the "reading" of a story, from naming things in the book to filling in parts of the story to telling the story themselves.

HOW CHILDREN DEVELOP LANGUAGE

All children progress through stages of language development, and while they may progress slower or faster than the child across the street, the sequence is consistent. We'll describe the progression for toddlers through kindergarten (age eighteen months through five) because these are the important ages for Active Reading.

Eighteen to Twenty-three Months

As children approach their second birthday, they can follow simple commands (get the juice, put the block away). They're learning simple verbs (eat, sleep) and are able to point to familiar body parts (nose, eye). They are starting to connect animals and the sounds they make and may give the animal's sound instead of the animal name (they say "moo" when they see a cow, for example).

During this time, reading with your child may involve pointing at pictures in the story and naming them or having the child point to simple pictures that are familiar to them; for example, pointing to the animals named in *Big Red Barn* by Margaret Wise Brown and talking about what noises the animals make or what each animal is doing.

Two to Three Years

Around thirty months, children may use fifty words, including some spatial concepts (in, on), descriptive words (big, happy), and pronouns (me, her). They are still able to say fewer words then they understand; a child may say fifty words but can understand far more. Their speech may be becoming more accurate or adult-like, but they leave off the ends of words. And they can answer simple questions using short (two- to four-word) sentences.

During Active Reading, they can talk more about the pictures and respond to questions like "What do you see on this page?" They can name familiar objects and pictures in books. At this point, children start retelling simple rhymes. For example, after reading the book *Brown Bear, Brown Bear* by Bill Martin, your child may be able to retell the story using felt animals. As your child retells the story, you may even hear her mimic the rhyme the same way she's heard you read it all those times.

Three to Four Years

At this point, children have gained lots of words that they'll use to talk about what they're doing each day. They're starting to group objects into categories (food, clothes, etc.). In addition to knowing the names of objects, they know what each is used for. Children at this age repeat phrases and sentences they hear and enjoy playing with language. They may recite poems or nursery rhymes and laugh at simple humor. They may like to talk about things that are silly to them. They are also starting to identify feelings, including talking about how characters feel and why.

Active Reading with a three- to four-year-old involves talking about what is happening in the story, encouraging the child to tell you what is happening in familiar books, and asking open-ended questions, like how characters are feeling.

Four to Five Years

In their preschool years, children can say as many as three hundred different words and can use verbs and verb tenses (ran, fell, pushing). They understand more complex questions and can describe how to do something that follows a sequence (e.g., making a sandwich). They are able to define words and list categories of items. They are starting to answer "why" questions.

Active Reading with four- to five-year-olds involves lots of whys and asking and talking through complex questions. Children at this age will be able to follow a simple plot, so talk about the events in stories. For example, when reading *Corduroy* by Don Freeman, you may have this conversation with a four-year-old:

> "Where does Corduroy live at the beginning of the story?"
> "In the department store."
> "That's right, and what happened to Corduroy?"
> "He lost a button."
> "What does he do to find his button?"
> "He goes up the escalator and tries to pull it off the mattress, but then he falls off."
> "Does he find his button?"
> "No."
> "How does he get a button?"
> "His friend Lisa gives him one."

In that exchange, the adult is helping the child retell the story through "Wh-questions" (Who? What? Where? When? Why?) that sequence the events of the story for the child.

As you read, encourage children to lengthen their sentences and provide them with more complex words. Also, encourage them to retell stories you have read together. As children progress in their storytelling, they start by reciting stories the exact way they heard them or how they experienced them during reading. Then they tell the same story with a new setting or with different characters. This reciting and retelling are ways that children start to build comprehension, test out story structure, and engage with stories in a new way.[1]

Five Years Old

When children start kindergarten, they have vocabularies between three thousand and five thousand words. They can follow three-step directions, tell stories using their imagination, and engage in longer conversations using sentences that are becoming more complex with more description. Active Reading with a five-year-old will consist of lots of why, what if, and how questions, as well as lots of connections to their own ideas and experiences.

Active Reading and Language

Age	Language Milestones	What to Expect When Active Reading
18–23 months	• Can say as many as 20 words but understands far more • Can follow simple commands • Uses simple verbs • Points to body parts • Connects animals and sounds	• Can point to and name familiar pictures in books
2–3 years	• By 30 months, they can say about 50 words • Understands spatial concepts • Understands descriptive words • Uses pronouns • Speaks in two- to four-word sentences	• Points to and names familiar and interesting pictures in books • Asks basic questions • Starts retelling simple stories and rhymes
3–4 years	• Can group objects into categories • Knows the purpose and use for common objects • Plays with language (may make rhymes • Repeats phrases and sentences • Identifies feelings • Identifies cause and effect	• Asks open-ended questions • Asks about character feelings • Starts to ask why questions
4–5 years	• Can say 300 words or more • Uses verbs and verb tenses (past tense, future tense) • Can answer complex questions, including why questions • Describes procedures	• Asks open-ended questions • Talks about events and the sequence of events in stories • Retells full stories
Kindergarten	• Has a vocabulary of 2,000 words or more • Follows three-step directions • Tells his or her own stories • Engages in longer conversations and complex descriptions	• Asks why, what if, and how questions • Makes lots of connections

What to Remember

• Children learn language quickly during their early years. From two-year-olds who are able to say short sentences, to kindergarteners who can carry on a conversation and tell complete stories, between the ages of two and five, children go through a period of rapid language learning.

• Active Reading supports children's language learning during this period by providing strong modeling and teaching of language, sentences, and vocabulary.

REPEATED READING

If you've been around young children, you know that they like to do the same thing over and over (your child's favorite phrase may be "More! More!"). For young kids, reading the same story over and over is especially important. Reading the same book again and again is about more than hearing the same story until they've memorized the words. It literally helps to build children's brains.

When children are young, their brains are ready to receive lots of new information. This information travels through the brain along the same pathway each time. Repeated reading builds kids' brains by strengthening the pathways between the cells. So every time the child says a word, reads a story, or engages in a conversation, neurochemicals are released that makes those brain pathways get stronger. Their brain recognizes this and holds onto the pathways in the brain that are strongest because of repetition, even when the brain may get rid of other, lesser used pathways.

The more often something is repeated, the more likely it will be remembered.[2] This also explains why skills that children learn when they are young are the skills that stick with them, whether that's riding a bike, learning letters, or learning how to swim.

In addition, repeated reading increases kids' language and vocabulary and allows children to start predicting the story and language in the story.[3] Reading a book over and over (and over) provides kids with opportunities to connect the story to their developing knowledge and remember more information that they can build on in future readings.[4] From your child's perspective, think of repeated reading as spending *more* time with something that you love. As long as your child wants to read a book, it's not boring for him (even if you tired of the storybook a month ago).

Repeated reading is about getting more from the same book. The first time you read a story with your child, you may point to and name things in the pictures. In subsequent readings, you'll be able to ask more questions and talk about more things in the story.

Think about it as digging further into the book. In the first reading, you may ask a lot of what questions ("What is this? What is he doing?"). Talking about what is happening and naming objects in the book will help your child learn the language that they need to understand the story when they read it again.

In a second reading, or when you have read the book a few times, you can start asking more open-ended questions, such as: "What's happening? What do you see on this page? Tell me what's happening here." This provides children with more ownership about what they can talk about and focus on as they read.

Finally, as you've read the story multiple times, you can start connecting the story to the child's world. Ask questions that start with "Do you remember . . ." or "Why is he doing this?" These questions help the child make connections between their life and the story, as well as between the start and end of the story.

How to Read a Book Over and Over

Repeated Readings	*Good Night, Gorilla* by Peggy Rathmann	*Corduroy* by Don Freeman
Ask What Questions	What animal is this? What is the gorilla doing?	What is this? (an escalator) Who is this? (a security guard)
Ask Open-Ended Questions	What is happening on this page?	What is happening? What is Corduroy doing?
Ask Connection Questions	What do you do when you want to go to sleep and someone is bothering you? Remember when we went to the zoo; what animals did we see?	Remember when you got your teddy bear; how did you get him? Remember when we were at the department store; what did we see?

📖
What to Remember

• Repeated reading is an important activity for young children. When you repeatedly read with children, it strengthens neural pathways in their brain, literally building their brains to enable them to become strong readers.

• Reading the same book over and over helps children learn and practice important language and skills.

• You can make repeated readings more fun by asking different types of questions the more you read a book. The first few times you read, talk about what you see; then talk about what is happening on the page and connections you can make.

PICTURE WALKS

Beth Murray had read *The Napping House* with her two-year-old daughter Esmè before, but she didn't spend as much time looking at the pictures until she started doing picture walks. When Beth and Esmè spent time studying the pictures in *The Napping House*, Esmè noticed things that Beth hadn't, like the little flea and the mouse on the bedposts and that the light in the bedroom was getting brighter and brighter on each page. A picture walk, or taking time to study the pictures, talk about them, and tell the story using the pictures, is one way to engage children in a new book or to find more in the images in a familiar book.

The goal of a picture walk is the same as the goal of Active Reading: to have a conversation about the book, in this case, the pictures. When you do a picture walk, you're not reading the words on the page but studying the pictures. This is why books with rich illustrations that give lots of details to describe, like David Shannon's stories (*Too Many Toys, Duck on a Bike, No David!*) and *Roller Coaster* by Marla Frazee, are great for picture walks. (Find more books that are great for picture walks in appendix A.)

Picture walks start a conversation about the book using the illustrations, which encourages children to take turns and practice important skills that they'll use when reading and talking about the story. For you, picture walks are a great chance to listen to your child's ideas and use their ideas to build their language. They also pique kids' curiosity about what might happen in a story.

Here's how to engage your child, or the children you work with, in a picture walk.

First, show your child the cover and ask them:

- What do you think the story will be about?
- What do you see on the cover?

Then, look at each page and ask questions about what they see with questions like:

- What is going on here?
- What do you see on this page?
- Who is this character?

Encourage them to make inferences based on what they see on each page:

- Why do you think this character is so excited?
- What do you think is going to happen next?

Encourage your children to provide whatever responses they think and don't give the story away. It's okay if their answers are wrong—they haven't read the story yet! Encourage them with statements like "That's a good idea" or "I didn't think of that."

After you've done a picture walk and are reading the words in the story, talk about what you saw in the illustrations and if there were any predictions you made that were correct or incorrect. This helps your child connect the conversations you had and gives them the practice of making and evaluating predictions.

QUESTIONS TO ASK DURING A PICTURE WALK

During a picture walk, you look at each page of the story before you read the words. Spend some time pointing to and naming objects or characters. Ask open-ended questions that encourage your child to notice things in the pictures, and explain what you notice and what that makes you wonder. There are picture walk questions that you can use with any book:
- What is happening on this page?
- What do you see on this page?
- Who do you think this is?
- Why do you think this character looks so sad (excited, happy)?
- Where is the character on this page?
- What just happened?

These are questions you can ask after you have done a picture walk and are reading the words in the book:
- What actually happened? We thought ___. Were we right? Why or why not?
- Was it a good idea for the character to do that?
- Now that you know what actually happened, why do you think the character looks so sad (excited, happy)?

A picture walk is a natural thing to do with a book that is new to you and your child, but it can also be a great way to revisit familiar books. Ask your child to describe the pictures and what they see on each page while you're revisiting a book you've read before and you may find, like Murray, that your child has noticed details that you'd overlooked or has a favorite part of the pictures that you didn't notice before.

Reading Wordless Picture Books

"This book has no words," three-year-old Saha says as she chooses *Journey* by Aaron Becker and hands it to me.

"That's right," I reply, "so we have to tell the story and talk about the pictures."

Saha opens the book and starts describing the first page. "The little girl wants to play, but her mom is busy, and her dad is busy, and her sister is busy," she says and points to the characters. "So she draws a door and goes through it."

"That's right; she draws a red door," I say, "and what does the girl see on the other side?"

"A forest," Saha says. She turns the page to see a picture of the girl emerging through a door into a forest that is lit with lanterns.

Wordless picture books are a great way to encourage your child to talk about pictures in books, especially if they're used to listening to you read and you want to encourage them to engage in more conversation. Talking about what you see in each picture, and making an effort to connect one picture to another, is enough to help your child understand the thread of the story. You can also apply the approach to repeated reading to help your child name objects in the picture, expand on their knowledge of the story, and connect to their world. (There is a list of wordless picture books in appendix A.)

What to Remember

- Picture walks are a good way to use book illustrations to introduce children to stories.
- During a picture walk, ask open-ended questions about the pictures (What do you see on this page? What is this?) and encourage your child to talk about the details in the images.
- Wordless picture books are a great way to involve your child in storytelling because they have to rely on the pictures to tell the story.

FILL-IN-THE-BLANK PROMPTS

Joel and his mother are reading *The Gruffalo's Child* by Julia Donaldson, a story about a small Gruffalo (an imaginary woodland beast) who goes in search of what her father has called "the big bad mouse." The Gruffalo's child meets three creatures (a snake, an owl, and a fox) in the wood, and each time she does, Joel's mother pauses for Joel to fill in the missing text.

"Aha Oho!" she reads and pauses.

"A trail in the snow," Joel fills in.

Joel's mother continues to read, stopping before the end of a sentence when Joel adds, "Big bad mouse!" He squeals and giggles.

Children need to practice saying words in order to learn them. Fill-in-the-blank prompts occur when the adult leaves off part of the text for the child to complete, as Joel's mother did in the example. Requiring children to say words increases their ability to understand and use the words they learn from books.[5]

Books with repeated phrases are ideal for this kind of participation; for example, filling in the rhyming words in the book *Rumble in the Jungle* by Giles Andreae or completing the repeating sentences in *The Napping House* by Don and Audrey Wood. Children can also fill in words in stories; for example, if they completed the sentence, "Then Trixie realized SOMETHING" in Mo Willem's *Knuffle Bunny*. Completing parts of sentences like this allows children to communicate that they understand how the story is read and that they understand what is happening in the book.

What to Remember

- Fill-in-the-blank prompts are when the adult leaves off parts of a book, like the end of a sentence or rhyme, for the child to complete.
- Asking children to fill in the blanks to familiar sections of text helps children practice saying words and phrases.

TALK MORE

The goal of Active Reading is to encourage children to talk a lot about the stories they read. The Talk More procedure is one way to get kids to talk about what they are reading. Through Talk More, adults model language for children, while children build their own skills.[6] Talk More involves a series of steps:

1. Ask your child a question or have them point to or name something on the page.

2. When your child responds, repeat what they say, and add descriptive words or additional information. This language that you add is important; it both affirms and expands on what they say. Make sure to explain if their answer was correct (yes, that's right!), and if it's not correct, provide them with the correct information (I think . . .).

3. Have your child repeat the full sentence.

4. Ask another question related to the story that continues the conversation.

5. Ask a question that connects the story to the child's world.

6. Praise and encourage your child throughout the interaction. Hugs, encouragement, and praise keep your child engaged and help them understand that they are doing good work.

For example, while reading *Corduroy* by Don Freeman:

1. Ask your child a question or have them point to or name something on the page: *"Where is Corduroy on this page?"*

2. *The child points to Corduroy, who is sitting in a department store case with other animals and dolls. "He's right there," the child says.*

3. When your child responds, repeat what they say, and add descriptive words or additional information. *"You found him! He's in a display case, the kind of case that we saw at the store we went to the other day."*

4. Have your child repeat the full sentence: *"Where is Corduroy?" you ask again. "In the display case," says the child.*

5. Ask another question related to the story that continues the conversation: *"Who is Corduroy with in the case?"*

6. Ask a question that connects the story to the child's world: *"Remember when we went to the store? What did we see?"*

The goal of Active Reading is to have a conversation about the story. Talk More provides a way to model strong language to your child and encourage them to lengthen their interaction about the story. It's a simple procedure, and after a while, it will become a habit and a way that you engage with your child when you read together.

What to Remember

• Talk More supports children's language development both by modeling language and by having children build and practice their own language.

• Talk More is all about encouraging your child to have a conversation about what they read.

READING TOGETHER

Children develop language fast! From your child's first word to their first explanation of all the things that happened at their first day of kindergarten, Active Reading builds kids' language by providing them with examples of language and support for their own communication. Reading the same book over and over, asking your child to fill-in-the-blanks while you read, using picture walks to introduce a story to your child, and using Talk More throughout picture book reading are all ways to build your child's language skills through Active Reading. In chapter 4, we will discuss how to implement the A of the ABCs of Active Reading: Ask questions.

How to Talk about a Book

Asking Questions

I open *Curious George* by H. A. Rey and start reading. "This is George . . ." In the picture, George is curious about a yellow hat on the ground. "What does George do?"

"He goes and gets the yellow hat," says Saha, three years old. She points to the image of George approaching the yellow hat.

On the page where George and the Man with the Yellow Hat are rowing to the ship, Saha points to the image of the ship. "That's a ship," she says.

"That's right; a ship is a big boat. How are they getting to the ship?" Saha points to the rowboat. "On a boat."

"That's right; they're traveling on the water in a rowboat."

In the picture, George stands on a ship deck. "What did George do?" I ask.

"He jumped and splashed into the water."

I turn the page.

"You're right; he fell right into the water, headfirst."

A few pages later, the illustration shows a fireman staring at a map with one spot lit up.

"What is that?" Saha asks, pointing to a picture of the fireman's map.

"That is where the firemen look to see where to go to fight the fire. But is it a fire?"

Saha shakes her head no.

"That's right; it's not a fire. It's a naughty little monkey."

For three weeks, Saha asked to read *Curious George* over and over again. During those three weeks, she pointed out increasingly familiar details in the story and learned how to retell the events. She talked about how firemen get calls and how George got caught but later escaped. She talked about how it was nice for the little girl to buy balloons for her little brother. The more she read, the more she was able to anticipate what was happening in the story and talk about how the events connected.

$\mathcal{T}$he goal of Active Reading is to have the child take over more and more of the conversation as you read the same book again and again, the way that Saha explained more and more of the story each time we read *Curious George*. The main way that this is accomplished is through asking questions.

Recall the approach to asking questions that we covered chapter 3. In this approach, the first time you read a story, you ask questions that focus on words you want the child to know and understand. For *Curious George*, that means asking questions like: "What is George wearing? Where is George now?" Then, when you read the book again (and again), you ask more open-ended questions that encourage the child to share what they want to talk about on each page: "What did George do next? What happened to the Man with the Yellow Hat?"

Also, in repeated readings, you ask the child to connect the story to their own life: "Have you ever been curious like George? Remember the time you were curious about what would happen if you put your teddy bear in the bathtub? What happened then?" Asking different types of questions and advancing the questions you ask so that they start easy and then become more difficult creates opportunities for children to engage with the book in different ways each time you read it. This also builds your child's knowledge the first few reads, then expands on their knowledge the more they read the story.

In this chapter, we will explain why asking questions is important, how it connects to children's later reading comprehension, and how to ask different types of questions during Active Reading.

ASKING QUESTIONS

It's important that young children are asked questions throughout the day. In preschool classrooms, adults do a lot of the talking. Conversations about behavior (How does that make Oliver feel?), daily routines (What do you want for lunch?), and following directions (Can you pick up the red blocks, please?) consume a lot of the day.[1] As a parent, you may find that much of your day involves questions that encourage or cajole your child to follow directions or think about their behavior.

This makes sense; there are a lot of things that have to get done every day and children are learning everything from how to complete new routines to how their actions affect others. Still, the way we engage kids in conversation is important. The way that adults talk to kids may make the difference between whether or not preschool has an impact on kids' language skills.[2] In preschool or at home, Active Reading provides an opportunity to engage kids in conversation in a way that goes beyond everyday conversation.

Asking questions is also something that good readers do when they read. As adult readers, when we engage with novels, the newspaper, or other text, we're constantly asking questions. As we read, we wonder: What will happen next? What is this about? What does it mean for me? Asking questions during Active Reading starts children on the same path to actively engaging with ideas, stories, and information.

Asking questions—starting with questions that have clear answers in the pictures or story and building to questions that do not have a clear answer—helps children understand and use language. Even young children can answer questions that ask them to make inferences, think critically about a story, and make evaluations, all skills that are critical to understanding what they read. Reading *Curious George*, questions that are evident in the pictures and words are those that ask about characters, settings, and details in the text. For example, what did Curious George find? (A yellow hat.) What happened to George? (He jumped into the water.) Where is George now? (In a jail cell.) Questions that do not have clear answers include those that ask children to make inferences or ask the child to bring together their knowledge about the world with the story to answer the question. For example, How does George feel? What does George want? What else could George have done? Should George be punished? Why or why not?

What to Remember

• Questions are one way that we engage with and experience books and stories. As good readers, we constantly ask questions about what we are reading.

• Asking questions—starting with questions that have answers that can be found right in the text and building to questions that require children to infer or think more deeply—help them understand and use language.

• Young children can learn to answer basic and more complex questions. We should be asking children lots of different types of questions each day.

SETTING THE FOUNDATION FOR READING COMPREHENSION: HOW CHILDREN LEARN TO UNDERSTAND WHAT THEY READ

When we engage children in conversation about books, we find out what they understand from the words and pictures in the story. As they build comprehension, children must first understand the words on the page, either those that are read to them or those that they read on their own. Then they must create an image or idea about what the words mean in sentences and paragraphs. This could mean constructing an image of the Quimby family eating breakfast together in *Ramona Quimby, Age 8* by Beverly Cleary, or it could mean a more abstract representation, such as understanding how Ramona feels when she has to entertain toddler Norma Jean.[3]

For example, read these sentences: *Jack looked out the kitchen window. He saw the headlights from Jane's car round the corner and pull into the driveway.* In your mind, you can see Jack at the window, perhaps he was doing dishes or cutting up vegetables for dinner. You understand that Jack was inside and that Jane was coming home. You can infer that it's nighttime and may have envisioned the sweeping of headlights. You may wonder what their relationship is. Is Jane coming home from work? How was her day? Is she exhausted or invigorated? A lot of reasoning went into imagining that simple scenario. While we read, we're constantly using information to create mental images and building on that image as we get more information.[4] For example, add the information: *Jack dried his hands on the dish towel and picked up the ring box.*

Now that you have added this information to your mental image, you can infer, from your knowledge of relationships, that Jack is about to propose. Now you may feel excited for Jane and Jack, especially when you read: *The garage door opened and Jane walked inside. She took off her coat and hung it on the hook. "What's all this?" she asked. Jack knelt down, flattening a few rose petal under his knees, and opened the ring box.*

Now what do you see? Have you imagined the kitchen table covered in rose petals with a special dinner simmering on the stove? Is Jack's heart flip-flopping with nerves? Does Jane have tears in her eyes and her hands on her heart in surprise? We could continue this scenario until Jack proposes and Jane accepts (or not, which would be a plot twist), but this shows how we use even simple sentences to create meaning that is both limited to the words on the page (we all imagined Jack in the kitchen) and expanded beyond the page (we combined our knowledge of relationships and emotions to infer what was in the ring box and what Jack was about to do). We created knowledge that extended our understanding of the scene and allowed us to predict what may happen (Jane will accept his proposal) and enjoy the emotion that comes with it (the excitement of seeing two characters finally get engaged).[5]

In the same way you made sense of the sentences above, asking questions during Active Reading helps children learn how to make meaning. For example, Monica McMahon read *Turtle and Snake Go Camping* with her son, three-year-old Jude. On a page with owls, McMahon asks Jude to count the owls on the page.

"Three, or there's two?" Jude replies.

"Well," says McMahon, pointing at the book, "I see yellow circles and I think those are owl eyes, so I see one pair of circles, two pairs of circles, and three pairs of circles. How many is that?"

"Three."

"'Run away!'" McMahon reads. "How do you think they feel?"

"Scared."

"Scared, yes, I think they feel scared, too. What do you think scared them?"

"Owls."

"The owls scared them."

In this reading, McMahon helped Jude understand how the illustrator was showing the owls (their eyes), which helped Jude create an understanding of how many owls there were. McMahon's questions helped Jude understand how to use the story, in this case the pictures of the eyes and then the words "Run away!" to better understand what was happening.

What to Remember

- When we read, we focus both on the literal meaning of what is happening or being explained and on more complex understandings that involve making inferences and predictions and other higher-order thinking skills.
- Asking questions helps us ascertain what children know and understand about the stories that are read to them. It also helps children talk about books and work with questions the way adults do when we read.

ASKING AND ANSWERING QUESTIONS: THE FOUNDATION FOR READING COMPREHENSION

As you read the words on this page, you use multiple skills developed over many years to help you. First, you understand each individual word and then maintain that understanding across sentences, paragraphs, and chapters. And you likely did it with minimal effort. When we read, we recognize the words on the page, build that knowledge from sentence to sentence, keep previous events and ideas in our immediate "working memory," and draw from our long-term memory to connect current text with what we previously read.[6] Comprehension is the purpose of reading, and it involves mastery of multiple skills for children to successfully understand what they read.

We've already discussed how language is important for reading comprehension. For beginning readers, children who are learning to read words on their own, there is not as much of a correlation, or connection, between reading words and comprehension. This is because beginning readers are not able to read or process what they read very efficiently.[7] They are still learning how to read words and hold meaning in their minds at the same time.

At this age, a child's ability to use language is higher than their reading ability. However, as children grow as readers, the importance of spoken language in relation to their understanding of what they read increases steadily through high school.[8] This means that as children apply their word-reading ability to reading on their own, their language skills become increasingly important to help them understand more difficult text.

The ability to answer questions is an important part of reading comprehension. Questions help children focus on and make sense of the story or text. Early research on Active Reading techniques found that when parents and teachers asked more questions, children were better at talking about the stories.[9] There are two main types of questions that we'll talk about for Active Reading: story questions and open-ended questions.

Story Questions

Story questions are the typical "wh" questions that you likely think about first: Who is in the story? Where is the story? What is this called? Story questions help children focus on story details and how stories are organized.

Stories are organized in a certain way. At the start, we are introduced to the characters, the setting, and the beginning events. There may be a problem that the character wants to solve. In the middle, we follow what happens to the characters, the decisions they make, and how they tackle the problem. And, at the end, any problems are resolved and the story comes to a resolution. We ask certain types of questions at different points in a story. There are some questions you'll ask only at the start (Who are the main characters?), while you'll ask other questions only as the story progresses (How did the character change?).

For example, in *Bunny Cakes* by Rosemary Wells, older sister Ruby wants to make a cake for Grandma's birthday. Little brother Max spills the ingredients, one by one, on the floor and then "helps" by going to the store to replace each one. But Max wants candy of his own and can't figure out how to communicate it to the grocer as he's not able to write words yet.

Throughout the middle of the story, Ruby gets increasingly frustrated with Max as he tips flour onto the floor, spills milk, and breaks eggs. Max, on the other hand, gets more and more creative and tries new ways to get his candy from the store clerk who can't read his scribbles. In the end, both bunnies succeed in creating a cake for grandma, who is thrilled. This story has a clear plot, with problems for both characters, and a story that progresses toward a resolution.

Children's understanding of story structure, or the elements of a story (characters, setting, plot, problem, resolution), is important for later comprehension, and it develops early.[10] By age three, children typically understand that what people want (motivation) causes human action, which is important for understanding how one aspect of a story impacts another (for example, how what a character wants impacts their choices).[11]

Story questions help children understand story structure by focusing on specific parts of a story. Using *The Story of Ferdinand* by Munro Leaf, here are some story questions that you could ask:

- How was Ferdinand different than the other bulls?
  He didn't like to run around or play fight; he just liked to sit and smell the flowers.
- What did Ferdinand like to do?
  He liked to sit quietly in the shade of a tree and smell the flowers.
- Why was his mother worried about Ferdinand?
  She didn't want him to be lonely.
- Why did the men come?
  The men came to find bulls to fight in Madrid.
- What happened when Ferdinand sat by the cork tree?
  He sat on a bee, so he looked very fierce.
- What happened when Ferdinand got to the bull ring in Madrid?
  He sat in the middle of the ring and smelled all the flowers in the lady's hair.

The purpose of asking story questions is to help the child focus on story elements and to engage your child in a conversation about the book. You may ask a story question on every page or every few pages, depending on the story itself and your child's interest. Sometimes, a child may want to talk a lot about the pictures and the details in a story. Other times they may want to sit and listen.

Retelling Stories

Retelling, or summarizing a story that they are familiar with in a logical order, is one of the first ways that children engage in deeper understanding of what they have read. In fact, a child's early ability to retell stories they have heard (or personal stories) is a good indicator of how well they will do in reading later in school.[12] Good retellings incorporate an explanation of what happened that is in sequence, a description of the characters and setting, and a description of the problem and solution. You can build your child's ability to retell stories, first by asking story questions, then by asking the child to retell longer and longer parts of a story. Also, ask your child to help you retell familiar stories when you are riding in the car or sitting at dinner. Ask: Who was in the story? Where were they? What happened? What happened next?

📖
What to Remember

- When we read, we use our ability to read words combined with our language skills to make sense of what we read.
- A child's language skills help them understand what they read and become more important as they learn how to read on their own.
- Story structure is the way that stories are organized, including all the elements that stories contain (characters, setting, plot, etc.). A child's understanding of story structure develops early and is important for comprehension.
- Story questions help children understand what is being read to them and draw their attention to important details in a story.
- Retelling a story is one way a child can show how well he understands what was read and is an important foundational skill for later reading comprehension.

Open-Ended Questions

Story questions are "closed" questions because the answers are in the text and will not change no matter how many times you read the book. Open-ended questions ask a child to think and use their own words to describe, explain, or interpret what is happening in a story. Open-ended questions are questions that cannot be answered with a simple "yes" or "no" response or just using basic information from the book. These questions ask your child to infer information, make predictions, and form opinions about the story.

Open-ended questions ask children to respond to a question that may have more than one correct or possible answer.[13] You ask an open-ended question without fully understanding what the child's response will be, though you may have an idea. These are valuable because they require thinking and extended responses and encourage conversation. These questions often start with "why" or "how" and require detailed description and explanation.

Some open-ended questions you can ask while reading *The Story of Ferdinand*:

- What kind of bull was Ferdinand?
- How was Ferdinand feeling?
- Why do you think the men were so excited to find Ferdinand?
- How do you think the other bulls felt when Ferdinand got taken away?
- What would you do if you saw Ferdinand in a meadow?

Another way to think of open-ended questions is that they "open" conversations. Through open-ended questions, we can engage children in making inferences, thinking about feelings, considering consequences, and expanding their ideas. Open-ended questions challenge children to think and be creative. They also challenge us to stop and wait because children may need time to think of an answer and to listen because we don't always know how children may respond. When asking open-ended questions, be sure to provide lots of time for your child to think, as many as ten seconds (which likely feels like a long time to adults).[14]

It may seem important to ask as many questions as possible when you read (isn't the goal to engage children?!), but for open-ended questions, it's not about how many but the opportunity for the child to respond that's most important.[15] Instead of asking lots of questions without time to talk about them, ask one or two questions that encourage lots of interaction using Talk More (chapter 3). This can increase the amount of learning that happens. When adults encourage conversation about a few complex questions, children learn more vocabulary than when adults ask lots of questions while reading.[16] There are different types of open-ended questions that will challenge kids' thinking: inference, prediction, consequence, compare/contrast, problem solving, and evaluation (table 4.1).

Inference Questions

When we read, or when children are read to, we are constantly creating meaning. Inferencing, or using knowledge combined with the text to create new knowledge, helps us build meaning from the text. We can make inferences at the sentence level. For example, *Amy poured cereal and milk in a bowl. She devoured her breakfast.* In that second sentence, we can infer that Amy's breakfast was the cereal and milk that she poured into the bowl, even though it doesn't say so explicitly. We've connected meaning between the two sentences.[17]

We also make inferences at the story level. For example, when we think about the theme of a story, or what the story is about, we use information from the beginning, middle, and end of the story to come up with the big ideas. Or we use information from earlier in a story to understand later information in the story. When reading *The Story of Ferdinand*, as we learn about Ferdinand's calm character, we can infer why he refuses to fight in the bull ring even though the author never tells us exactly why.

When we read, we don't make every possible inference. Instead, we make inferences that are necessary to understand the story, and many of these are made automatically. In particular, strong readers will make more causal inferences, or inferences that involve connecting information from earlier in the story with new information. Young readers make inferences using the same skills that adult readers do, though young readers may not do this spontaneously. So when adults ask questions and talk children through making inferences, it teaches kids how to make inferences on their own.[18] Our ability to make inferences also depends on our knowledge. As children develop knowledge of the world around them, they are able to make more inferences (chapter 6).

Prediction or What's Next Questions

Prediction questions ask readers to use their knowledge of the story to anticipate what will come next. We ask prediction questions at the start of the story or before important events in the story. For example, before reading *Ferdinand*, we could ask: What do you think this story will be about? In the middle of the book, we could ask: What do you think Ferdinand will do when he gets to the bull ring?

The trick with prediction questions is following up. After you ask a prediction question and your child has given you an idea (or you've suggested one), return to the child's idea after you have read a few more pages. Then, either notice that the prediction was correct or talk about what actually happened and how it was different than your prediction.

Consequence or What If Questions

Questions that ask "what if" help students think about different ways the same character or story information could be different. These questions engage children in thinking about point of view, or who is telling the story. For example, for *Curious George*: What if George hadn't found the hat? What if the Man with the Yellow Hat hadn't found George on top of the stoplight?

Compare and Contrast

Questions that ask children to compare and contrast ask them to think about how things are similar and different, such as when you compare two characters: How is Ferdinand similar to and different from the other bulls?

Compare and contrast questions also provide a frame for connection questions that ask your child to compare and contrast their experiences with those in a book (chapter 6).

Problem-Solving Questions

When stories have a problem, problem-solving questions ask children to think about alternative ways to solve the problem. These are questions like: What else could the character have done? What would have happened if they had solved the problem that way? Problem-solving questions encourage children to use their imaginations and construct new story endings or possibilities. Thinking about *Bunny Cakes*, you could ask: What does Max want? What is the problem that Max has to tackle? What does he do to solve his problem?

Evaluation Questions

Evaluation questions ask children to form an opinion about whether something that happened in a story was right or wrong. Reading *Bunny Cakes*, they may evaluate whether or not it was right for Ruby to be so mad at Max after he spilled flour on the floor; or, in *Curious George*, whether it was okay for the Man with the Yellow Hat to take George with him on the ship.

Young children are learning how to understand and formulate responses to open-ended questions. So, while they are important to get kids thinking about stories, children may also need help to answer them. If your child isn't able to answer questions that you ask, that's okay. This is where you step in. Providing your own answer to an open-ended question is a way of showing your child how you think and how they can organize their own thinking.

Types of Open-Ended Questions

Type of Question	Purpose	Example from *The Story of Ferdinand* by Munro Leaf
Inference	Encourages children to combine knowledge with the text to create new knowledge	Should the men have known not to take Ferdinand to the bull ring in Madrid?
Prediction: What's Next	Encourages children to use their knowledge of the story to think about what could logically happen next	What do you think Ferdinand will do when he gets to the bull ring? What makes you think that?
Consequence: What If	Encourages children to use their imagination to create new scenarios	What do you think Ferdinand would have done if he hadn't sat on a bee? How would the story be different?
Compare/Contrast	Encourages children to see how ideas, characters, situations, and other aspects of stories are similar and different	How is Ferdinand different than the other bulls? What do you think the other bulls think of Ferdinand?
Problem Solving	Encourages children to analyze a situation and propose a solution	How did the men solve the problem with Ferdinand in the bull ring? Was there anything else they could have done?
Evaluation	Encourages children to think about whether or not a situation was appropriate	Did the men do the right thing?

What to Remember

• Open-ended questions challenge kids to think about what they've read and how it connects to what they read before and their own experience and knowledge. They "open up" a conversation.

• There are various types of open-ended questions that we can ask: inference, prediction, consequence, compare and contrast, problem solving, and evaluation.

• When we ask open-ended questions, the goal is to have a conversation, so it is better to ask a few open-ended questions while reading and have enough time to use Talk More to discuss each.

• If you are reading with a child and he or she isn't able to answer an open-ended question, share how you would answer the same question to show how you think.

TALK ABOUT A BOOK

The point of asking questions is to engage your child with the book. Ask many story questions, a few open-ended questions, and use Talk More (chapter 3) to create routines around talking and listening with your child while reading that will develop their comprehension skills and love of reading. Kids love to be engaged and listened to. Asking questions during Active Reading encourages your child to have conversations that you won't have any other time during the day, which is why the A of the ABCs of Active Reading is so important. Next, we examine the B of the ABCs: Building Vocabulary.

• 5 •

Building Vocabulary

How to Teach Words in Books

*M*onica McMahon reads *Spaghetti in a Hot Dog Bun* by Maria Dismondy to Jude, then almost three years old. In the book are words her toddler has never heard before: *kindness, poodle, disgusting, hollered, poofy, monkey bars, courage.* While she reads, McMahon repeats the words so her son will hear them pronounced correctly. She explains each word in different contexts or talks about what the word means. "Monkey bars are a piece of play equipment that children use to swing," she says, "like monkeys swing on trees." She relates the words to other words he's heard in books or experiences he's had: "A poodle is a type of dog. Like our dog—he's a beagle."

Reading picture books has given Jude exposure to words that aren't used in everyday life. And, yes, he uses the words he learns from books when he's talking to his parents, but he also develops critical thinking skills by talking about language. Picture books, says McMahon, help anchor abstract nouns and concepts. As they read, books spark conversations about words. When reading picture books about an octopus, McMahon talks about the quantity of eight and the prefix "oct." "How many tentacles does an octopus have? How many sides are in an octagon?" Her son can see the tentacles and count the sides on an octagon, as well as visualize other, less concrete concepts, like feelings and actions.

A child's early vocabulary is an important predictor of later reading success. In the years before elementary school, children learn words at a fast pace.[1] In this chapter, we will discuss how children learn words through Active Reading, by using the pictures to define words, creating kid-friendly definitions, asking questions, and making connections with the words.

BUILDING VOCABULARY: A POWERFUL TOOL

Ask any parent or early childhood educator who has spent the day with a young child and they will tell you: young kids love to talk. By the time they are in preschool, children have transitioned from saying a few words to putting sentences together, even creating words of their own. At one point, you may have been able to list all the words your child knew, until one day when your child said a word you didn't remember using at home and you realized that your child's vocabulary had outgrown your mental list.

Children's early word knowledge is a predictor of future reading success.[2] When children have a strong vocabulary, they are able to infer meaning when they read words and sentences.[3] For example, a child who knows the words *ax, hog, weak, decided,* and *unfair* will be better able to understand the beginning scene of the classic children's novel *Charlotte's Web* by E. B. White, in which Fern learns that a runt has been born and that her father is going to the hog house to take care of it. They will be able to anticipate the possibility that a pig is going to be killed and will infer how distraught Fern feels about her father's plan.

The sheer number of words that children must learn to read well is staggering. By the time they start middle school, children must know tens of thousands of words in order to read proficiently.[4] Of course, this includes simple, common words that adults will use often (*no, sit, down, wait*) as well as more complex words that are used in writing (*glee, timid, mischief*) and words that are useful for understanding specific texts or topics (*crustacean, octopus, democracy, waterfall*).

A child's most important vocabulary milestone may occur long before middle school. Children have very different vocabularies at the start of preschool. Decades ago, two researchers at the University of Kansas, Betty Hart and Todd R. Risley, documented the "word gap."[5] They calculated that young children in professional families heard as many as thirty million more words than children in low-income families. This initial language knowledge was important; they also found that this difference in the size of children's vocabulary predicted later reading comprehension in third grade.[6]

Closing this "thirty-million-word gap" has become a rallying cry among early childhood advocates, but it is better viewed as a metaphor for understanding how children can vary in their reading development rather than a rule or assumption about a child's vocabulary based upon their background.[7] It is important to note that even though parental factors (education level, socioeconomic status, home environment) do make a difference, home literacy practices and a parent's attitude, expectations, and goals for his or her child's reading have an impact on a child's vocabulary and language, as well as enjoyment of reading.[8]

In fact, a study of more than three hundred kindergarteners found that children of low-income households whose parents engaged them in a variety of literacy activities at home before they started school outperformed their peers in higher-income households whose parents engaged in fewer literacy activities.[9] How parents and children interact is so powerful that home literacy activities can account for 12 to 18.5 percent of the variance in children's language scores.[10] *This means that a child's vocabulary is greatly impacted by how his or her parent interacts with him or her.* This is encouraging because, as parents and teachers, the words we expose children to and how we help them use those words are within our control—regardless of where we live or what language we speak at home.

Word learning and vocabulary building start early and compound over time. Think about word learning as a snowball; when you start packing a snowball, once you have a few snowflakes, it's easier for more snowflakes to stick to the ball. In the same way, once you learn a few words, more will "stick" as you add more words to your vocabulary. Having a large vocabulary provides children with more to build on; the more words children know, the faster they are able to learn new words.[11] Also, as children build their vocabularies, they learn new words and, as those words become familiar, they learn more about those words, like when Jude and his mother talked about how octopi and octagons both have eight of something. This depth of knowledge about words creates a richer understanding of how words work and how we can use them.[12]

What to Remember

- Vocabulary is important. A child's early vocabulary predicts their later reading ability.
- Children start learning words and building their vocabulary early, and they must continue adding to their vocabulary throughout their school years.
- The larger a child's vocabulary, the faster they can learn new words.
- The adults in a child's life have an important impact on the child's vocabulary, regardless of other factors such as family income or the language they speak at home.

FINDING RARE WORDS IN BOOKS

As McMahon found in her experiences reading *Spaghetti in a Hot Dog Bun*, picture books are a powerful way to expose children to words they don't hear in typical conversation. Thinking about the conversations that likely occur at home or in an early childhood classroom, many words we use to get kids to cooperate, engage them in pretend play, and teach them about daily experiences are often the same from day to day. While ongoing conversation is important, picture book reading provides an opportunity to develop children's language in a way that simply won't happen just by talking more during everyday interactions.

Of course, each child will build his or her own vocabulary based on words that he or she is exposed to. For example, a child whose parent is a chef may learn the words *cleaver, dice,* and *sauté* sooner than a child whose parent is not a chef. Even as each child is building his or her vocabulary, there are some common themes to the types of words that children learn from books.

Words can be divided into three categories: Common Words (Tier 1), Rare Words (Tier 2), and Knowledge Words (Tier 3). Common Words, or Tier 1 words, are the most basic form of any word and are used most often in everyday language (*yummy, blue, hat*). Rare Words, or Tier 2 words, are used more often in books and less in conversation and are often synonyms of Common Words (*delicious, navy, beret*). These are the types of words that make picture books so fun and interesting to read. Knowledge Words, or Tier 3 words, are content-specific (science words like *atom, microscope,* and *prehistoric*).

Children are exposed to Common Words through everyday conversation and interaction. Children already hear most Common Words at home, so we don't have to teach them. Children are exposed to Knowledge Words when they get interested in a topic and explore it, picking up lots of new vocabulary along the way. When a child takes an interest in dinosaurs and is able to explain the difference between a triceratops and a brontosaurus, she is using Knowledge vocabulary. They also learn these words when they study a subject in school like the life cycle of butterflies (e.g., *larva, chrysalis, metamorphosis*).

Having a vocabulary full of Rare Words is what separates proficient from struggling readers in terms of vocabulary. Rare Words are high-frequency words that are more common in writing than everyday speech: *endure, despise, contrast, adjacent, crucial.* The irony is that although adults with high school diplomas and college degrees know many Rare Words, they normally use mostly Common Words when they talk to each other. And without prompting, adults mostly tend to use Common Words when talking with children. One of the richest sources of Rare Words is picture books.[13] When we do

Active Reading, part of the focus is on teaching those Rare Words to children who may not learn them any other way.

Types of Words in Picture Books

Book	Common Words (Tier 1)	Rare Words (Tier 2)	Knowledge Words (Tier 3)
The Little Red Hen by Paul Galdone	Little House Nap Clothes Floor Cut Red	Cozy Porch Snooze Housework Mend Ripe	Mill
Caps for Sale by Esphyr Slobodkina	Head Back Gray Street Tree Angry	Peddler Wares Cap Upset Trunk Disturb	
Mama Built a Little Nest by Jennifer Ward	Little Mama Wall Roof Sky Feet Bed	Nest Sturdy Wee Snug Cobweb Craggy Ledge	Fledge Talons

*These are a selection of words from each book as examples of the types of words that can be found in picture books.

📖
What to Remember

• Children must learn different types of words: frequently used Common Words; complex Rare Words used more often in writing than speaking; and Knowledge Words for specific topics.
• Children's picture books are one of the best sources for children to learn Rare Words.
• Active Reading is a way for caregivers to find and teach Rare Words.

BUILDING VOCABULARY FROM BOOKS:
REPEATED READINGS AND CONVERSATION

Children learn more words from books when we intentionally teach them. Multiple studies have shown that children learn only about 15 percent of the new words they encounter in a story if the words are not explained to them. However, this jumps to about 40 percent if we take the time to introduce and explain new vocabulary words.[14] Even better, children tend to remember the new words that they learn when we stop to talk about them.

Once kids have been taught words, they get practice using words through conversation. This back-and-forth exchange using words (think "serve and return") helps children connect words to pictures, define words, and understand words in context. In addition to conversation, repeated reading of books and talking about the same words over and over help solidify and deepen children's knowledge of words.

Active Reading, conducted one-on-one (or between a few children and an adult) between a parent, caregiver, teacher, or reading buddy and a child, provides the most specific and deep opportunity for rich vocabulary learning.

More Reading, More Words

One way to ensure that children are getting practice with words that we've taught is through repeated reading. Children need to read the same book multiple times to learn words from it. Reading a book over and over (often more than four times) provides both more exposure to the words and multiple opportunities to practice with those words.[15] Repeated readings also allow time for children to advance their understanding from an initial understanding of a word to a deeper comprehension.

For example, when you first read *Bear Feels Scared* by Karma Wilson, you may point at the picture of Bear by a tree to show your child how Bear is huddling. Re-reading the book, you may talk about how huddling means to crouch down and talk about the different ways you could see huddling (in football, when your child huddles in a hiding spot during hide-and-seek). There's a lot to talk about even with just that one word, and kids need multiple opportunities to spend time talking about the nuances of words and how they're used in books.

One-on-One Conversations

Mira, a three-year-old, joins her mother on the couch to read *Bunny Cakes* by Rosemary Wells. Mira has read *Bunny Cakes* before and knows the bunny characters, Max and Ruby. Mira's mom opens the book and starts to read. "'It was Grandma's birthday. Max made her an earthworm birthday cake.' What's an earthworm?"

Mira points to the picture that shows Max playing in a pile of dirt.

"That's right," her mother says. "Max is playing in a pile of dirt. Earthworms are bugs that live in dirt. Where do earthworms live?"

"Earthworms live in dirt," Mira repeats.

"And they are long and squirmy," her mother says. "Can you squirm?"

Mira wiggles on the sofa.

"That's it!" her mother says and keeps reading.

One-on-one conversations, like the one that Mira and her mother had while reading *Bunny Cakes*, are the most valuable for language learning because they provide the most specific, targeted, and individualized language use. As children learn words, they focus first on the important features (the picture of Max playing in the dirt), then use attention and conversation about the word (the mother's description of a worm) and other clues to make meaning of words.[16] Talking with kids one-on-one also provides opportunity for children to receive feedback about whether they are using words correctly.

Through one-on-one conversations, adults can adjust their responses to what the child already knows. If Mira had seen worms the day before, her mother might have referred to that experience to define "earthworm." If an earthworm is something that Mira's mother knows she has no experience with, she could take time to show Mira images of an earthworm or go outside and dig in the dirt in search of tunneling earthworms.

Small-Group Conversations

Even in child-care settings, engaging in one-on-one interactions with books is important and a focus of this book. However, one-on-one conversations are not always possible. Perhaps you have multiple children, or a you're teaching and a small group of children all want to hear the same book. Children *can* learn new words when reading in small groups, and it can be helpful to have other kids in a group when learning a new word. For example, in one study that looked at how teachers engaged children with words while reading, children who read in small groups learned more words because they talked with one another.[17]

Here is one example of how this could look in an early childhood classroom:

Ms. Allen sits in front of a small group of four-year-olds. She holds *Bunny Cakes* up and waits for her students' attention. When the group is settled, she starts reading. "'It was Grandma's birthday. Max made her an earthworm birthday cake.' What's an earthworm?"

Billy raises his hand. "It's a long dirt bug."

"It does crawl in the dirt, and it is a bug. Has anyone else seen an earthworm?"

Michelle raises her hand. "My brother said they come out after it rains."

"Yes, we often see earthworms after it rains. They are long bugs and they look like tiny snakes. Do you think we'd want to eat an earthworm?"

The group shakes their head no.

What to Remember

- Children learn the most words from books when adults introduce and explain word meanings as they read.
- Repeated readings of books help vocabulary learning "stick" by providing multiple opportunities to practice and talk about the words.
- Talking about words by explaining them and helping children connect the word to the book, their experiences, and their knowledge help children learn word meanings and how to use them.
- Children can learn words through one-on-one or small-group conversations.

BUILDING VOCABULARY THROUGH ACTIVE READING

Active Reading involves four strategies to build vocabulary from books: using the pictures, creating kid-friendly definitions, asking questions, and making connections.

1. Using the Pictures

Often, you can help your child define a word using the pictures. This may mean pointing to a character's expression to help show what the word *yawn* or *giddy* means. Or you may point to the objects in a picture to define the words for various types of gardening tools (*trowel, rake*). Using the picture helps your child see what the word means by immediately connecting the picture to the word.

2. Creating Kid-Friendly Definitions

Creating a kid-friendly definition provides a way for your child to understand a new word using words they already know. To create a kid-friendly definition, talk about the word using language that you know your child knows. Then refer to that kid-friendly definition each time you encounter the word.

For example, in the book *The Gruffalo's Child* by Julia Donaldson, you may teach your child the word "boulder." After pointing to the picture of the Gruffalo's child sitting on a boulder, you say, "A boulder is a big rock." This kid-friendly definition uses concepts (big) and words (rock) that the child is familiar with. It is also a general definition that the child could use if they saw the word "boulder" in another book.

3. Asking Questions to Build Vocabulary

Asking questions about Rare Words gets children thinking and talking about the words in books. There are different ways that adults can ask questions while reading, but simply asking questions is an effective way to build vocabulary.[18] There are two types of questions that we think about when asking questions during Active Reading: Right Here (or literal) questions that ask what a word means using information in the book and Stop and Think (or inferential) questions that ask what a word means using knowledge or information from sources other than the book you're currently reading.

Different types of questions engage children in different types of thinking (chapter 4 has more information about types of questions). When young children are asked both Right Here (literal) and Stop and Think (inferential) questions about words in a story, they show greater vocabulary growth compared to children who are not asked questions when reading.[19] Even though young children will learn more literal language than inferential language, meaning that they will learn the names for things faster than they will learn deeper meanings, preschoolers can still develop inferential language through the storybook reading experience. Knowing how to think about and answer both types of questions will help children understand what they read when they move into school and learn to read on their own. During Active Reading, asking a variety of question types helps children think about the words in books in different ways.

Right Here Questions

Right Here (literal) questions refer the child to the story to learn or use the word. For example, using the book *Swimmy* by Leo Lionni:

- "Swift means fast. Can you show me moving fast with your hand?"
- "A gulp is a big swallow. The big fish gulped the little fish. Can you point to the big fish that gulped?"

- "The medusa was made of rainbow jelly. Where is the medusa? What colors is the medusa?"

Stop and Think Questions

Stop and Think (or inferential) questions ask the child to use information from other stories, their experience, or through more abstract thinking that does not come right from the book to answer the question about the word. For example, using *Swimmy*:

- "The big fish is swift. What else can be swift? What can the fish do because he is swift?"
- "What else can you gulp? What else might the big fish gulp?"
- "The medusa was made of rainbow jelly. Why might it be rainbow? Why might it be good for it to be so colorful?"

Asking Questions about Words in Books

Book	Word	Literal Question	Inferential Question
Caps for Sale by Esphyr Slobodkina	Wares	What is the peddler carrying on his head?	Why might the peddler be carrying his wares on his head?
	Caps	Caps are another word for hat. What colors are the peddler's caps?	Why does the peddler carry his caps stacked up on his head?
Mama Built a Little Nest by Jennifer Ward	Moss	What color is the nest made of moss?	Do you think moss is soft or hard? Why?
Cricket Song by Anne Hunter	Footfall	What is the whippoorwill listening for?	How do you think the whippoorwill is feeling? How does the footfall of the fox make her feel?

Another way of thinking about questions is to consider what you are asking the child to do. Right Here and Stop and Think questions are a way to adapt Active Reading as your child develops their vocabulary reading their favorite books. Right Here questions introduce children to words and are effective with younger children (ages two to three) who do not have as advanced vocabularies and are learning what words mean and how to use them.[20] Stop and Think questions challenge children to think more about the words they are learning by using the words in new ways, making connections between the story and their own lives.[21]

The First Time You Read a Book

When you are reading a book with your child for the first time, introduce two or three new words by asking questions about the words using the pictures as references. For example:

Reading *Bunny Cakes*, Mira's mom turns to the final page. "'Grandma was so thrilled,'" she read. "Thrilled means that she was happy. Who was thrilled?"

Mira points to the picture of Grandma Bunny.

"That's right," her mother says. "Grandma was happy or thrilled to get two cakes for her birthday."

In this example, Mira's mother used a Talk More prompt (chapter 3) to confirm and add to Mira's answer and focus on the word *thrilled* at the same time. Over time, Mira's mom could ask more Right Here questions, such as "How does Grandma feel?" to make sure that Mira knows what *thrilled* means before she expects Mira to answer Stop and Think questions, like: What might make me feel thrilled? When did you feel thrilled?

Reading a Book for the Second, Third, or Hundredth Time
As your child learns more about the overall story, they can think more deeply about how the word fits into the story. And the more often a child reads the same book, the more they can answer Stop and Think questions.

Reading *Bunny Cakes*, Mira's mom turns to the final page. "'Grandma was so thrilled,'" she read. "What was she thrilled about?"

"To get cakes."

"That's right; she was thrilled to get two cakes. Who were the cakes from?"

"Max and Ruby."

"They were from Max and Ruby. Has your grandmother ever been thrilled to get something from you?"

Mira nods.

"You made her a card last week; I bet she was thrilled to get that card."

"Thrilled to get the card," Mira replies.

"That's right."

Here, Mira's mother connected the word to the context of the story and to Mira's own experience. After reading *Bunny Cakes*, Mira's mother might use "thrilled" throughout the day, when Mira brings her a picture she's drawn or when they are playing pretend.

4. Make Connections with Words

Once your child has talked about a word in a book and understands the word, encourage him to make connections for how he might encounter the word in other places.

For example, if you taught your child the word "boulder," you might try to find boulders during a visit to the park. Or you could find boulders in other picture books, like the big black rock in *The Snail and the Whale* by Julia Donaldson and in the scenes in *Cricket Song* by Anne Hunter.

📖

What to Remember

• Asking questions about words helps children think about and use words they are learning.

• There are two types of questions that can build vocabulary: Right Here (literal) questions help children define words in the story by often relying on the pictures. Stop and Think (inferential) questions ask children to use the book along with their experiences and knowledge to answer a question.

• During Active Reading, varying the type of questions asked about words helps children engage with new and familiar words in different ways.

• Once a child has learned a new word, help them connect it to experiences and other stories.

BUILDING VOCABULARY AFTER READING: TALKING BEYOND BOOKS

Talking about words outside of the immediate story is important. In fact, how much adults talk about words can be as important as reading books with those words in them.[22] There are ways to talk about words that children learn from picture books after a reading session has ended: vocabulary-building activities, talking about words, connecting books to books, and connecting experiences to books.

Vocabulary-Building Activities

Active Reading increases the number of words a child knows and uses, and kids can use those words outside of reading time to continue to expand and strengthen their vocabulary. When preschool teachers engaged kids in Active Reading, then provided activities that reinforced the words from books, children learned more words than those who were only read books.[23] For example, when children were read *The Carrot Seed* by Ruth Krauss, about a boy who plants a carrot seed and patiently waits for it to sprout and grow into a carrot, after reading and talking about the book, the children participated in a center where they played with seeds and gardening tools. The gardening center helped kids use the words they had just learned in what is, for kids, a real–life context, pretend play.

Combining Books and Activities to Build Vocabulary

Book for Active Reading	Vocabulary Words	Questions to Ask	Centers or Activities to Do
The Little Red Hen by Paul Galdone	Wheat Fine Delicious	What does wheat look like? How did the bread smell? What other foods smell delicious?	Make bread together. Go to a bakery and watch bakers busy in the kitchen. Show your child things that are "fine" like sand and "coarse" like gravel.
Swimmy by Leo Lionni	School of fish	The fish swim together in a school. How many fish are in a school of fish? Swimmy is one fish in the whole school of fish. Can you find Swimmy?	Move around your house like you are in a school (close together). Cut fish out of sponges and create schools of fish by sponge painting.
Mama Built a Little Nest by Jennifer Ward	Nest	Find the nests on each page. What is inside each nest? How big is the nest? Where is the mommy bird?	Take a walk around your neighborhood and find nests in trees. Use blankets and pillows to create a nest to put stuffed animals in.

Talk about Words

When McMahon reads with her son, she takes advantage of the words found in books to connect them to broader language. She may talk about synonyms of a word, that *disgusting* means the same as *nasty* and *gross*. Or, if something is the opposite of *disgusting*, it could be *delicious* or *tasty*. Talking about words that have similar meanings (synonyms) and words that have opposite meanings (antonyms) is one way to talk about words that expands children's vocabulary by creating connections between words they know and new words.[24]

Another way to talk about words is by identifying when words have multiple meanings.

Ms. Taylor reads *Mr. Tiger Goes Wild* by Peter Brown to a small group of children. When the word *wild* appears in the story, she stops and asks her students, "What does wild mean?" The first time, a horse is saying, "Now children, please do not act like wild animals."

"Wild means that they should not act like animals that live in the jungle, like a lion or tiger," explains Ms. Taylor.

The next time it is mentioned, Mr. Tiger wants to loosen up and to be wild. "What does he want to do?" Ms. Taylor asks.

"He wants to go crazy," Ben suggests.

"That's right; he wants to really act differently, doesn't he?"

The third time the word comes up, Mr. Tiger has "a very wild idea." "Here, wild means that his idea is not normal; it is a very creative idea," Ms. Taylor explains.

As the class continues to read the book and return to the book, Ms. Taylor continues to talk about the slightly different meanings of the word *wild*.

When you read, you'll find words that have multiple meanings and books that play off of the various meanings that one word can have. Point these examples out to your child, and think of the ways you could use those words in your own way.

Connect Book to Book

As you read, you'll find the same word in multiple books. Take this opportunity to talk about how the same word can be used by different authors.

Charles sits on his mother's lap. His mother turns the page in *The Napping House* by Audrey Wood. "'A snoozing cat,'" she reads. "Oh, Charles," she observes, "the cat is snoozing in this story, just like the cat was snoozing in *The Little Red Hen*. Where is the cat?"

Charles points to the cat asleep on top of a pile of people and animals. "And what is he doing?"

"Sleeping."

"That's right; he's snoozing."

"Snoozing."

"Like the cat in *The Little Red Hen*. Snoozing must mean like taking a nap."

Connect Words to Experiences

Connect experiences in your life or your child's life back to vocabulary in the books you've read together. For example, after no one comes to help you clear the table or clean up, talk about how you feel frustrated, like the *Little Red Hen*. Or explain that you're seeing footprints in the mud like the Gruffalo's child saw footprints made by animals in the snow. It's not necessary to plan events that force an encounter with vocabulary (for example, planning a visit to a museum); just paying attention to and naming how the experiences, feelings, animals, and items in books pop up in everyday experiences is enough to carry on the conversation.

What to Remember

• After a child learns words from a picture book, continuing to use the words and talking about them is important to continue vocabulary development.

• Talking about how words are connected (synonyms and antonyms), various meanings that one word can have, and connecting back to books you've read with children are all ways to continue building vocabulary after Active Reading.

BUILDING VOCABULARY AS CHILDREN GROW

As children develop, how they engage with Active Reading will change, as well as how they use and connect with words. With young children (ages two to three), the focus may be simply on defining words and helping children understand how words are portrayed in books. Children may point to or say one-word responses to show that they know a word: how the mouse is "snoozing" in *The Little Red Hen* or how the smile on Grandma Bunny's face shows that she is "thrilled" in *Bunny Cakes*. But, as children advance, asking Stop and Think questions, encouraging children to use more words that they've learned from books in everyday language, and talking about how words are similar or different build kids' vocabulary and prepare them to learn even more words. As a child's vocabulary develops, he or she will start referring to the words in books, telling you that they are *thrilled* or explaining that they want to travel in a *school* just like Swimmy.

How Active Reading Changes over Time

Book	Word	Beginning First Reading	Developing Repeated Reading	Advanced Repeated Reading
The Gruffalo's Child by Julia Donaldson	Creature	Point to the creatures on the page.	Ask a literal question: What creature is the Gruffalo's child talking to?	Ask a high-demand question: What other creatures have you seen today?
Caps for Sale by Esphyr Slobodkina	Monkey	Fill in the blank using the pictures to help your child identify the words that are missing: "On every branch sat a . . ." (point to the monkey).	Ask a low-demand question: How many monkeys are there?	Ask an inferential question: How do you think those monkeys feel?

Active Reading takes advantage of the Rare Words that we find in picture books to build kids' vocabulary and sets the foundation for later reading success. In chapter 6, we will explore more deeply how and why making connections to the child's world is an important component of Active Reading.

· 6 ·

Make Books Bigger

Connect to the Child's World

*O*ne of the joys of parenting or teaching young children is experiencing their "firsts." Everything is a first for a young child: the first time they make tracks in snow, the first time they visit a laundromat, the first time they make muffins. It's all new. With each experience, children build knowledge about what happens in the world (that snow falls in winter and feels cold), how things happen (snow falls from the sky), and even why (snow happens when the air is so cold that water vapor freezes).

As they develop, children draw on and build from this knowledge to understand more complex ideas. Using the snow example, they might be able to anticipate a snowstorm when the temperature drops and dark clouds fill the sky or understand that an author might use a snowstorm to create a scene that keeps all the characters inside.

The C in the ABCs of Active Reading—Connect to the child's world— aims to make books and stories into broader learning experiences for kids: first, by connecting what kids read about to their immediate experiences, by teaching them about the world around them and how it works; also, by teaching them how to connect information within and across stories; and, finally, by building background knowledge, information that kids will use and develop as they read on their own.

In the same way that teaching your child new words through making connections (chapter 5) doesn't have to involve expensive trips or lessons, Connecting is not about creating expensive and time-consuming experiences that mirror the ones your child has read about. Instead, it's about helping your child see the connections between what they are already doing and what they have read. It's also about knowing how making connections helps kids grow as readers. In this chapter, we will cover how to Connect to your child's

73

experiences, how stories shape kids' ideas and behavior, and how to build background knowledge.

MAKE CONNECTIONS TO CONSTRUCT MEANING

Connecting to your child's world means helping your child build bridges between what they read about in books and their everyday experiences, and vice versa. Making connections makes the experiences in stories and the information in books come alive for kids. A child may be ecstatic to feel the snow fall—plop!—on top of their head, just like it fell on Peter's head in *The Snowy Day* by Ezra Jack Keats. He may be excited to talk about how washers work during a visit to the laundromat after reading Don Freeman's *A Pocket for Corduroy*. Or she may want to talk about the time she picked fruit after reading *Blueberries for Sal* by Robert McCloskey.

Connecting to your child's world is all about building knowledge. This is accomplished, partly, by making connections between children's prior experiences and what they read. It's sort of like Lego bricks, connecting individual bricks to create a larger structure over time. There are different connections that you can make during and after storybook reading. Using Active Reading, you'll make connections to your child's experience, knowledge, and text he or she has read.

We want children to get in the habit of making connections while they read. Reading requires children to connect individual pieces of information, and good readers constantly make connections between what they are reading, what they have read, and what they already know.[1]

Connecting helps children create mental images of what they are reading about,[2] whether that is visualizing a character who is sad or creating an image of what happens when two cells divide. Then they must connect information from sentence to sentence to understand what is happening, either adding new information to what they already know about a story or adding new facts to what they are learning about. As they read fiction, they must follow the story from scene to scene across a book, making connections from the beginning of the story to the end.[3] If they are reading nonfiction, they must connect new information with what they previously read. Making connections during Active Reading helps children get into the habit of drawing from what they know to understand new ideas, concepts, or information. In Active Reading, we ask questions that help children make those connections with experience, within the story, and to their prior knowledge.

CONNECT TO EXPERIENCES

Saha opened the book *Maisy Goes to Preschool* by Lucy Cousins. On the first page, Maisy arrives at preschool and puts her coat on a hook. "Where do you put your coat at your school?" I ask.

"In a cubby," Saha replies.

While reading, we talk about how Maisy's day at preschool is similar to Saha's. Maisy likes to play outside; they paint and eat snacks. Maisy takes a nap, but Saha does not. Saha feels excited to go down the slide, and her favorite outside equipment is the teeter-totter.

When you read books with your child, you may connect to experiences that are exotic (taking a family trip abroad), exciting (visiting the zoo), or common (going to daycare). Whatever children connect with, connecting to your child's world helps them see books as relevant to their lives, while building their understanding of events, places, feelings, and ideas.

You can help children make connections from their experience to the books you read together by asking questions that focus them on what is happening in the story and then on what has happened in their life. Reading the book *Jesse Bear, What Will You Wear?* by Nancy Carlstrom, you could ask: What is Jesse Bear wearing? What are you wearing? How did you choose your clothes this morning? Or when Jesse Bear "wears" his food for lunch: What is Jesse Bear "wearing" at lunch? What foods do you "wear" at lunch?

In Active Reading, we connect to the child's world by asking questions that ask children to remember when or think about what they've done in similar situations. To build these connections, it's important to read books about an experience before and after it happens or read "around" the event. Then ask Remember When and What Would You Do questions to help your child make important connections.

Read Around Events

Preschoolers are all about experiencing the here and now. Time is an abstract concept that kids don't grasp until elementary school, and preschoolers, already an egocentric bunch, are still learning about how time passes (which any parent who has tried to get out the door on time will attest to). Connecting to experiences makes reading relevant for children. When you connect a story to an experience that you have planned for the near future, like a holiday or family event, read both before and after the child's experience. Before the experience, first read the book with the child to build vocabulary and knowledge about what may happen. After the event, read the book again to encourage the child to talk about her experience and how it was similar to and different than what she read about.

Before a family trip to the beach, Saha and her little sister, Neina, read books about the ocean, including *Hello Ocean* by Pam Muñoz Ryan. They talked about what they wanted to do at the beach (digging in the sand) and what they would see (seagulls, waves). After their beach trip, the girls read *Hello Ocean* again, this time talking about what they did at the beach (dug in the sand, watched seagulls, stood in the waves) and how the beach they visited was different than the beach portrayed in the book (there was no tidepool at the beach the girls visited). The next time Saha and Neina encounter a beach in a book, they will have greater background knowledge because of their prior experiences in and out of books.

Remember When?

When reading a book that is about an event that your child has experienced, help them connect by asking questions that start with "Remember when?" (Remember when we went camping? What did we see?) Then follow up with a conversation about how your experience was similar to or different from what happened in the story.

What Would You Do?

Often, stories teach children about the world and, in that way, teach children how to behave and think.[4] Reading books about friendship, for example, may show your child ways that friends behave. We think about what a friend needs (*A Sick Day for Amos McGee* by Philip Stead). We appreciate our friends, even when friendship is not always perfect (*My Friend Rabbit* by Eric Rohman). It's important to judge friends by their character (*Big Al* by Andrew Clements). Children learn how to act toward one another through what they see in stories. Active Reading can help this by helping your child understand what is happening in the story through your conversation and their interaction with the book.

Help your child connect with and learn from stories by asking questions about when your child was in the same situation a character was, when they felt the same way a character did, and how your child handled it. This uses the story as a springboard to help your child problem solve situations in his or her own life and uses stories as a way to show your child how situations can be handled.

For example, if a new baby is coming into the family, you can read *The New Baby* by Mercer Mayer and ask: What did Little Critter do with the new baby? What do you do with your baby? (Or what will you do with your new baby?) How does Little Critter feel about the new baby? How do you feel about your new baby? Talking through how a character handled a big life event can help your child think through ways to handle it and experience the connection that makes reading relevant in general.

What to Remember

- Connecting to experiences makes reading relevant for children. It also provides an opportunity for children to think about how they are similar to and different from what they see in books.
- When possible, connect books to a child's experience by reading books before and after an experience. This helps prepare children to learn during the experience before it happens and encourages them to think and talk about it afterward.
- Encourage your child to connect your reading to experiences he's had by asking questions about things in the book that he has done (Remember when?) and how his experiences were similar to or different than those in the story (What would you do?).

CONNECT WITHIN STORIES

As children read, they are constantly making connections. One way they do this is by making connections between what happened in a story and what just happened a few pages before. This helps children maintain comprehension as they read. There are two ways to help your child connect within stories: showing how events within a book connect from one page to the next and connecting across stories to show children how stories can be similar.

Connect within the Story

Making connections within a story helps children see how stories are developed and how we can build understanding of what the text is about by using information the author gave us just a few pages before. For example, at the end of the story *Wolfie the Bunny* by Ame Dyckman, Wolfie hugs Dot and Dot says, "Come on, little brother, let's go home and eat." This is a big change for Dot, who was afraid of Wolfie at the start of the story. You can help your child connect the end to the start of the story by flipping between the pages and asking questions such as: How did Dot feel about Wolfie at the beginning of the story? How does she feel now?

You may also flip between pages to help children connect one event to another. For example, in *Fancy Nancy* by Jane O'Connor, when Nancy slips on her shoes while carrying parfaits, you may want to flip back and forth between the two pages so that the child can connect the two events and talk about cause and effect. What made Nancy fall? What happened when she fell?

Connect Story to Story

Making connections from story to story helps children see similarities and differences in books. Over time they'll make connections of their own. When you are reading, look for these different types of connections that you can make from story to story.

Character to Character

Look for characters that are similar from one book to the next. Characters may have similar traits, for example, the trucks in Virginia Lee Burton's books *Mike Mulligan and His Steam Shovel* and *Katy and the Big Snow* each like to do work. You might also compare and contrast the behaviors of Max in *Where The Wild Things Are* and David in *No, David!* When you notice similarities between characters, talk about how the characters are similar and how they are different.

Setting to Setting

Your child may notice books that take place in the same location. *Knuffle Bunny* by Mo Willems and *A Pocket for Corduroy* by Don Freeman both take place in a laundromat. When you read those books, talk about what happens at the laundromat that is the same in each book and what is different.

Events

Events in two books may be the same; books may deal with the same topic (getting a new sibling or moving to a new town). In this case, talk about what happens and how the characters dealt with their feelings, like how Peter felt about his new baby sister in *Peter's Chair* by Ezra Jack Keats compared to how Little Critter handled the same situation in *The New Baby* by Mercer Mayer.

Ideas

Multiple books often explore the same or similar ideas. For example, in *Kitten's First Full Moon*, a kitten mistakes the moon for a bowl of milk. In *Happy Birthday, Moon*, a bear mistakes the moon for a friend. Sometimes books explore similar ideas from different perspectives. For example, *The True Story of the Three Little Pigs* tells the story of *The Three Little Pigs* from the wolf's perspective. You can compare and contrast how the wolf and the pigs tell the same story.

How Stories Are Organized

Some books have familiar patterns that you will notice. The books *Away We Go* by Migy and *The Mitten* by Jan Brett both center around an object—a hot air balloon in *Away We Go* and a mitten that is stuffed full of animals until it explodes in *The Mitten*. In this case, you can connect the two stories by asking: What happens to the animals? Which animal comes in last and then what happens to the balloon or the mitten? What is the same about each book? What is different?

When you read stories, you'll also connect events at the start of the story to those at the end. Questions like: Why do you think the character did that? Why do you think that happened? and What happened first, next, and last? are all good ones to help children see that events in stories are connected. You may even flip back in the story to see what caused events or what clues the illustrator put in the pictures to help you anticipate what will happen next.

What to Remember

• Connect within stories by helping children understand how events early in the story impact later events.

• Connect story to story by talking about similarities and differences you see in characters, settings, events, and other aspects of stories.

BUILDING BACKGROUND KNOWLEDGE

In October, Saha was three years old, and I checked out a series of books on fall trees. Reading through the books, *My Leaf Book* by Monica Wellington, *Dappled Apples* by Jan Carr, and *Leaf Jumpers* by Carol Gerber, we talked about the types of leaves and how to describe them (gingko leaves have a fan shape, oak leaves have points), why leaves change color in the fall, and the parts of leaves (veins and stems).

One autumn weekend, we walked around our neighborhood collecting leaves to name and glue into Saha's own leaf book (a bunch of paper folded and stapled together into a booklet). Saha learned that leaves turn colors and fall from the trees in autumn, that different trees have different types of leaves, and that we can learn what kinds of leaves there are by studying them. She also learned a few specific types of leaves that she pointed out throughout the fall. The reading we did and the talking about leaves we saw outside our own house built her background knowledge about leaves and autumn.

Active Reading strengthens kids' background knowledge by involving them in learning information from books as they answer questions (What is happening to the trees?) and learn new words (maple leaf, stem). In many ways, asking questions and teaching children new words contribute to their background knowledge.[5] Every time you talk about a book or experience you help your child build new background knowledge about that topic.

Background knowledge is all the information that we have and use to understand new information that we get from conversations, stories, text, and other media. Think of background knowledge as what we bring to the table when we interact with someone or something. The amount of information that we already know or have experienced about a topic determines just how well we can engage with it.

Think about a topic that you know a lot about. It might be a sport, something to do with your job, or a hobby that you like. Talking with someone who also knows about this topic will be more engaging and stimulating for you than talking with someone who knows little to nothing. For me, this could be long-distance running. I used to train for and run long-distance races (though not very fast). Through years of distance running and racing, I can talk about the ins and outs of training in the "lingo" of running. I can carry on long conversations about training programs and schedules, when and how to use a foam roller, when to stop to fuel during a marathon, and which fuels to use.

I am drawn to books about running and stories about runners when I peruse bookstore shelves. When I read about races or running, I apply what I know to better understand new information about the sport. That's the point of background knowledge—not to know something about every subject, but to be able to apply the knowledge we do have to help us learn new information. For children, building background knowledge helps them understand and learn from what they read.

Background Knowledge and Learning to Read

When children start reading on their own, the amount of background knowledge they have about a topic affects how well they understand what they read.[6] Children who know more about a topic better understand text about that topic compared to children who do not know a lot about the same topic.[7] For example, if two children picked up a book about baseball, the child with more background knowledge about the game of baseball is more likely to understand and enjoy the story or text. As children grow, they must build a broad knowledge base that will help them understand what they read.

Also, having a strong base of knowledge helps children understand what they read more accurately. In one study, children with a stronger knowledge about science better understood a text about science and made fewer inaccurate conclusions.[8] Building background knowledge helps children accurately assess and examine new information to determine just how to add it to their knowledge base.

Finally, children use background knowledge to make inferences while reading. When children make inferences, they bring what they already know and combine it with new information they learn from a story to create new meaning that is not explicitly stated in the text.[9] For example, when a child reads the book *Knuffle Bunny* by Mo Willems, when they get to the part where Trixie is trying to communicate with her father who does not understand her because she is talking baby talk, children can use knowledge about how babies communicate along with their previous experiences of not being understood to better understand what is happening and how Trixie feels.

Building Background Knowledge through Active Reading

Building background knowledge is about more than amassing lists of facts that kids can rattle off (though some kids won't hesitate to tell you everything they know about their favorite topic, and this is okay). It's about helping kids develop networks of information.[10] Think about it as a web—having information about a topic and seeing how that information connects to information kids know and new facts and ideas. Here are a few ways to build your child's background knowledge during Active Reading.

Help Your Child See Connections

Before you read a book, ask your child what they already know about the topic. Perhaps they've already read about the character before or they saw a panda at the zoo and know that pandas eat bamboo. Then, while you read, talk about the new information presented in the book, as well as how it connects to what your child already knows.

Questions about similarities and differences, and the reasons behind this, help children think about this. When reading a book about astronauts, you may talk with a child about gravity. On one page in the book, a picture shows astronauts sleeping in bags that are attached to the wall. You may connect this to your child's knowledge that there is no gravity in space. Then compare it to how you sleep by asking: How do astronauts sleep? How do you sleep? How would you sleep if you were an astronaut? Why?

Talk about Words in Categories

Teaching words in categories helps children start to make connections that are important for using vocabulary as background knowledge while reading.[11] You can do this while Active Reading or in your general interactions. While reading, you may talk about animals in a story, grouping all the predators or prey into groups. Or you may have your child cut out images from a supermarket advertisement and sort the foods into categories (fruit, vegetables, cereals).

Read Informational Text and Read Widely

Informational or nonfiction text is great for building background knowledge (see appendix A for nonfiction book ideas). If your child is interested in a topic, reading widely, or reading lots of books about that one topic, is a great way to build background knowledge. The more you read about a topic, the more you can connect from book to book, showing your child how information she learns in one book helps her understand information in a new book, even as your child develops facts and information about the topic itself.

Use Multimedia

William Crain and Clover (four years old) read *Room on the Broom* by Julia Donaldson. "Do your friends help you?"

"Yeah," Clover responded.

"It's good to have friends to help, isn't it?" He continued reading until the characters came upon a caldron. "Do you know what a cauldron is?"

Clover shakes her head no.

"It's like a big black pot," Crain explains. "You know who uses a cauldron? Zecora," he says, referring to *My Little Pony*, one of Clover's favorite TV shows. "Then she mixes the poison joke in to help the ponies."

"They thought she was going to cook Apple Bloom."

"That was funny," says Crain. "That's a cauldron. It was used by people who are doing magic."

In this case, Crain used Clover's prior knowledge of *My Little Pony* stories to help her understand the idea of a cauldron. As the child's parent, you know what your child already knows and has had experience with. She may have knowledge about how the world works (the types of trucks they will see on the highway), what is supposed to happen in certain situations (when you push someone, they will be upset), and facts that she has learned through conversation (pumpkins grow from seeds, trees turn colors in autumn). Just like connecting Lego bricks, all this prior knowledge that they have gotten from talking, asking questions, and even watching television becomes the general knowledge that children use to connect and understand relationships between characters, events, and other ideas in text.[12]

Television shows and electronic media resources can be a great way to show your child information that they would not be exposed to any other way. For example, a child who is interested in animals may benefit from watching animals in their native habitats, something that is often best done from the comfort of their couch. When children watch shows or video clips about something they are interested in, help them connect their new knowledge by talking about what they saw and putting it into categories. After watching a video about bears, you could ask: What did you see all the bears do? Is there something that only panda bears do?

What to Remember

• Background knowledge is all the information (facts, ideas, and knowledge) that we have and bring with us when we read text. Background knowledge helps us understand new information and understand it accurately. Background knowledge is also important for making inferences about what we read.

• The point of background knowledge is to be able to apply knowledge we do have to help us learn new information.

• Strong readers consistently make connections between their background knowledge and what they are currently reading.

• The amount of background knowledge a child has affects his or her reading comprehension.

• Making connections between your child's prior knowledge and stories helps children understand new information that they are presented with in text.

• Connect the book to what children know and to the background knowledge they have gained from talking with you, watching TV, and other methods. This builds kids' general knowledge and helps them see how what they already know can help them understand new ideas and information.

CONNECT TO YOUR CHILD'S WORLD

Connecting to your child's world is about more than talking about all the things your child has done; it's about helping him recognize and use knowledge to better understand what you read together now, so that he can better understand what he reads in the future. Connecting makes books relevant for kids, builds their background knowledge, and teaches them how to handle real-life situations.

Chapters 4, 5, and 6 have focused on the ABCs of Active Reading, which are all about building the skills and knowledge kids need to understand what they read (vocabulary and language). In the next chapter, we will cover how to help build your child's ability to hear, identify, and manipulate the individual sounds in words through Active Reading. This is called "phonemic awareness," and it's a critical early skill that will help prepare your child to learn to read in school.

· 7 ·

How to Talk about Sounds

Building Phonemic Awareness and Letter Knowledge through Active Reading

Reading *Bear Snores On* by Karma Wilson, a book we have read hundreds of times before, Saha stops me after the first page. "*Bear* and *lair*," she exclaims. "They rhyme!"

"That's right," I reply. "What else rhymes with *bear?*"

Saha thinks for a moment. "*Hair.*"

"Yup, and *fair.*"

"You're right," she tells me.

Finding rhyming words in texts like *Bear Snores On* is an important way that Active Reading can promote and build young children's understanding of sounds and how sounds make up words. This understanding, of how sounds are made into words and how we can change sounds within words to make new words, called phonemic awareness, is an important skill for children to start learning before they start school.

*P*reschoolers love to play with language by singing silly songs, finding words that start with the same letter or sound, and naming rhyming words. Active Reading is a way to teach and build kids' language, vocabulary, and comprehension. It's also a way to help reinforce important early reading skills that children should master before or as they are learning to read words on their own. Active Reading is a way that adults can teach and strengthen kids' knowledge of letters and letter sounds. As in the ABCs of Active Reading (chapters 4, 5, and 6), the focus here is not on having children read on their own, but in using books to start conversations, in this case about words, sounds, and language.

We've already discussed how Active Reading supports kids' understanding of concepts of print and print knowledge (chapter 2). This chapter will provide an overview of phonemic awareness, one of the core skills that children must have in order to learn to read on their own. Then we will discuss how to reinforce and strengthen kids' phonemic awareness through Active Reading. We'll also cover building letter knowledge, another important reading skill. Although the main focus of Active Reading is to grow your child's vocabulary and language skills, in this chapter, we will also cover how children learn to read words and how you can incorporate teaching letter sounds and letter names while reading with your child.

WHAT IS PHONEMIC AWARENESS?

Words are made up of sounds, or phonemes. Each word has at least one phoneme (some words, like *I* or "eye," have only one phoneme), and most have more than one phoneme (think about the words *cat* "c-a-t" or *love* "l-u-v"). The focus of phonemic awareness is on these phonemes or sounds rather than the letters in the words.

Phonemic awareness has nothing to do with letters or the spelling of words. For example, the word *whale* has five letters but only three sounds / wh/ /long a/ and /l/. As this example shows, the number of sounds and number of letters in a word do not always match up. Children who are skilled at hearing, identifying, and manipulating the individual sounds in words can play with words, changing the beginning and ending sounds to make new words. For example, a child who knows the sounds in the word *whale* can rattle off other words that sound like *whale* but begin with a different sound: *pail, rail, sail, tail, mail, veil, kale, trail, snail.* From that list, it's clear that phonemic awareness is focused on the sounds in words, not their spelling.

Why does this matter? Before children learn to read words, they need to be able to hear differences and similarities in words (when they identify or create rhyming words), put sounds together (blending), pull words apart into sounds (segmenting), and play with words by changing the sounds in words to make new words (manipulation). Together, these skills make up a child's phonemic awareness ability and will help children apply sound patterns later when they learn how to read. For example, when the child learns that "wh" together makes its own sound and that a letter "e" at the end of a word makes the vowel long instead of short, they can apply that knowledge to understanding how to read the word *whale* on their own. It will also help them to learn how to sound out other words that follow a similar pattern: *male, tale, sale, pale, bale, kale.*

As we learn to read, we progress from sounding out words that we can decode, or read, using the sounds in the English language (rat, sand, sheep) to being able to read them automatically, or without thinking about each individual sound. By the time we are skilled readers, we primarily read words automatically, without having to stop and sound them out. But as children develop the ability to read, they must learn first that letters and combinations of letters make sounds and that those sounds combine to create words.

When Do Kids Need to Learn to Read?

Hearing your child read his first words aloud is a milestone, for you and for them. It may happen as early as preschool or some time in kindergarten or first grade. In school, you can expect children to be taught how to read words starting in kindergarten and continuing into second and even third grade. The important thing for preschool children (ages two to five) is not that they are reading words on their own, but that they have strong phonemic awareness skills, or an understanding of sounds and how they work, that they can apply to letters when they learn to read. This, combined with kids' vocabulary knowledge, helps children understand the words they have sounded out, leading to reading comprehension.

Learning phonemic awareness doesn't require paper and pencil; it doesn't even require letters to play with. Children develop phonemic awareness by playing with language. Activities like singing silly songs, chanting nursery rhymes, listing off rhyming words, and clapping the number of syllables in a word (the word *snowman* has two syllables, "snow" "man") all build phonemic awareness. The games that children play, from singing "Down by the Bay" to making silly compound words (what if you combined the words "snow" and "wagon"?), prepare children to learn to read.[1]

In fact, phonemic awareness is one of the greatest predictors of how well children will do in reading in the first years of school.[2] Active Reading is an opportunity to build your child's phonemic awareness by playing with the sounds, words, and language you hear in books. Again, it's not about teaching children how to read words on the page but about helping them listen, play with, and experience language.

Revisiting Joint Attention

We've discussed how Active Reading, when you are reading one-on-one with a young child, is not a lesson in the formal sense. We are not requiring children to do anything or learn anything specific. Rather, the goal is to capture their attention and build language skills by following their lead and having a conversation based on what interests them in a book.

Part of this is adults responding to the child's interests, or joint attention (chapter 2). The same idea applies to phonemic awareness. The best time to talk about the sounds in words and engage in activities that help children create rhymes, segment words into sounds, and blend sounds into words is when the child is interested in it. If your child isn't interested in telling you words that rhyme with *bear* or more words they can think of that start with /a/ like *apple*, it's okay to stop and ask them what they do want to talk about or do next.

📖
What to Remember

• Children start reading words on their own anywhere between preschool and early elementary school. However, a skill they develop earlier, phonemic awareness, is a strong predictor of how well they will read in early elementary school.
• Phonemic awareness is the ability to hear and manipulate the small sounds in words. You'll notice your child developing phonemic awareness when they identify rhyming words, change one sound in a word to create another (changing the first letter in *fox* to make it *box*), combine sounds to make a word (/s/ /a/ /t/ makes the word *sat*), or pull words apart into sounds (the word *bone* has three sounds /b/ /long o/ /n/).

ACTIVE READING TO BUILD PHONEMIC AWARENESS

As you read books with your child, look for words that you can pull apart. A good place to start is breaking compound words into syllables, so separating words like *snowman*, *housecoat*, and *rainstorm* into smaller words ("snow" and "man"). After your child has gotten good at that and is learning their letter sounds, you can pull small words, like *hop*, *sat*, and *miss*, into individual sounds.

Here are some ways to build phonemic awareness while reading with your child. These activities are broken up into beginning activities, those that you can do with a child who is just learning about sounds (two to four years old), and advanced activities, those that you can do with a child who has more experience working with sounds (four and five years old).

Beginning Activities

These activities are best for young children (ages two to four) who are just starting to work with sounds.

Think about Patterns

Read books with word patterns, like *Going on a Bear Hunt* by Michael Rosen, and encourage your child to repeat the patterns along with you. The pattern could be a repeating paragraph, as in *Going on a Bear Hunt*, or a repeating sentence or word. (This is the fill-in-the-blank prompt, discussed in chapter 3.)

Separate Syllables

Knowing that words can be separated into parts is important and comes before segmenting words into sounds. Look for words that you can separate into meaningful segments, such as compound words. In the book *Snowmen at Night* by Caralyn Buehner, talk about the word *snowman*, what each word means, and what they mean together.

Words that Sound the Same

Help your child see rhymes (when two words sound the same at the end, like *whale* and *snail*) and alliteration (when two words start with the same sound, like "happy hippo") by looking for similarities and differences in words. Read rhyming books, like *Sheep in a Jeep* by Nancy Shaw or the *Llama Llama* books by Anna Dewdney, and say the words that rhyme. For example, the words *sheep*, *steep*, and *leap* all rhyme because they end with the same sound. Reading *Some Smug Slug* by Pamela Edwards, you could point out that the words *summer*, *Sunday*, *strolling*, and *soil* all start with the /s/ sound.

Say Silly Words

Creating silly words that rhyme with real words is a fun way to practice phonemic awareness. Using the book *There's a Wocket in my Pocket* by Dr. Seuss, you can talk about the silly words that Dr. Seuss makes up for everyday objects, then make up your own.

Advanced Activities

These activities are best for children who are already able to rhyme and talk about sounds in words (ages four and five).

Word Counting

While reading, turn the book toward you, so that the children cannot see the pictures. Tell them to listen to what you are going to read and to count the words. Then read a sentence at a time and have them count the words they hear. To start, you may draw a line on a piece of paper for every word you say. You can also do this with sentences they tell you. Ask your child to tell you a sentence, draw a line for every word they say, then have your child count the number of words in their sentence (and add a drawing to go with it!).

Syllable Counting

Help children count syllables in words by modeling how to clap or count the syllables that you say. Start with two-syllable words, then build up to three-syllable, four-syllable, and longer words. You can separate the syllables by clapping during each one or tapping your head, shoulders, knees, and toes when you say each syllable. When you come across a new word or a word that is long, stop to figure out how many syllables it has. You may start by counting syllables in your child's and his or her friends' names.

Sound Counting

When a child can count the syllables in words, start showing them how to hear the sounds in words. Choose a small word at first (*me*, *key*) and pull the word apart into individual sounds (m-ee, k-ee). Focus on the sounds, not the letters, in the word. You can use the same clapping and tapping strategies to count the number of sounds in each word. Remember, the goal here is not to hear all the letters, but the sounds. Don't worry about correct spelling, which will come later as your child learns common spelling patterns.

Beginning Sounds

The first sound in a word is called the *onset* of the word. /C/ is the onset of "cat" and /s/ is the onset of "snap." Children are able to identify the onset sounds first. Ask your child what sound they hear at the start of a word. You may say the word slowly to help them distinguish the individual sounds at first.

Put Words Together

The ability to break words into sounds (segmenting) and then put sounds together to make words (blending) is the most obvious phonemic awareness skill that children use when they read on their own. As adults, we use our segmenting and blending skills when we encounter new words (try to read the word *sesquipedalian*, which means to be long-winded, without breaking apart and blending some of the letters or chunks). Encourage children to practice breaking words down into individual sounds (segmenting) by using the pictures in books. Point to a picture and ask the child if the image is a /ddd/og, a /llll/og, or a /ssss/og, drawing out the first sound so that they can hear it.

Sound Talk Strategy

The Sound Talk strategy[3] is a more structured way to teach letter and word patterns through picture book reading. First, choose a storybook that has words with a specific sound pattern to teach. For example, you may teach words rhyming with *sheep* using *Sheep in a Jeep* by Nancy Shaw. Then plan to teach the word pattern while reading the book.

During the first reading, you identify and name the word patterns that are in the book. Reading *Sheep in a Jeep*, you would point out that all the rhyming words have "eep" at the end.

Then, as you read the book over and over, ask questions about the parts of the rhyming words. For *Sheep in a Jeep*, you could talk about the beginning sounds of each word: What sound does *jeep* have? What about *keep*? What about *leap*? You may also talk about rhyming: What other words rhyme with *sheep*? Can you make up a silly word that rhymes with *sheep*? And you may have the child say each sound in the word slowly to count the sounds (segmenting): Let's say that slowly. Sh-ee-p. How many sounds do you hear?

Because this is a listening activity, you're not worried about spelling patterns (the "eep" in *sheep* vs. the "eap" in *leap*)—it's all about listening for the same sounds.

What to Remember

- Talking about words and sounds, including finding rhyming words, counting syllables in long words, and finding words that start with the same sound, helps students develop phonemic awareness.
- Phonemic awareness is an auditory or listening skill, and when you engage your child in phonemic awareness practice, focus on saying the sounds and listening for the similarities and differences in words, not the letters themselves.
- There are ways to introduce a young child (ages two to four) to phonemic awareness, such as using the fill-in-the-blank prompt with books that have a pattern, separating syllables, finding words that sound the same, and creating silly words.
- Children who have had more experience with phonemic awareness (ages four to five) can do more work with phonemic awareness by counting words, counting syllables, or counting sounds. They can identify the beginning sounds in words and blend sounds together or pull sounds apart.
- Sound Talk is a formal strategy that can be used at home or in the classroom to teach phonemic awareness using picture books that have lots of words that can be compared and discussed.[4]

TEACHING LETTERS THROUGH ACTIVE READING

Knowing letter names at the start of kindergarten is an important skill. In fact, children's letter knowledge (how many letters they could identify and write when told the letter name) in kindergarten was a strong predictor of how well the child read in fourth grade.[5] Letter names are what we call each letter (letter A, B, C, and so forth). Letter sounds are the basic sounds that each letter makes (letter A says "a" as in apple, for example). (The two tables below have information about how to teach kids vowel and consonant letter sounds.) We've already covered how to teach your child important print knowledge and print concept skills through Active Reading (chapter 2).

Teaching letter names and sounds through Active Reading involves pointing out letters and pictures of words that start with the letter you've identified. For example, reading *LMNO Peas* by Keith Baker, have your child point to or trace the letter A, then point to the acrobats, artists, and astronaut peas in the illustration. (There is a list of alphabet books in appendix A.)

You can also have your child find all the letter As (or Bs or Cs) on a page. Start with the first letter in their own name and then branch out from there. Finally, you may ask your child to find pictures that start with the letter sound in a book you're reading. Simply focusing on the letters that you find in books will teach your child that letters have names and sounds and that they can learn every one of them.

Vowel Sounds
Use this table to teach your child the correct letter sounds for the vowels.

Vowel	Example Word for Short Vowels	Example Word for Long Vowels
A	Apple	Ape
E	Egg	Eek
I	Igloo	Ice
O	Octopus	Oak
U	Umbrella	Unicorn

Consonant Sounds
Use this table to teach your child the correct letter sounds for the consonants.

Consonant	Sound	Example Word	Consonant	Sound	Example Word
B	/b/	Bug	C	/k/	Carrot
D	/d/	Dog	F	/f/	Foot
G	/g/	Go	H	/h/	Hand
J	/j/	Jump	K	/k/	Kitten
L	/l/	Lamp	M	/m/	Mom
N	/n/	Nose	P	/p/	Pull
Q	/koo/	Queen	R	/r/	Rat
S	/s/	Seal	T	/t/	Toad
V	/v/	Violin	W	/woo/	Water
X	/ks/	Fox	Y	/yee/	Yellow
Z	/z/	Zebra			

When you say letter sounds, only say the sound of the letter. Try not to add an extra breath of air that adds an "uh" sound. For example, the letter B says /b/, not /buh/.

What to Remember

• Letter knowledge, or the number of letters that a child can name, is important. It is one of the predictors of later reading success.

• Teach letter knowledge while reading with your child by reading alphabet books and talking about the letters and words or by having them find different letters as you read. Letters that are in their name are always good letters to start with.

• Children must learn letter names and letter sounds. Use the tables above as a reference when you are teaching your child letter names and sounds with words they can use to remember each sound.

HOW DO KIDS LEARN TO READ WORDS?

Even knowing that the focus of kindergarten and first grade is all about teaching kids how to read, you may want to teach your child letter names, sounds, and even how to read a few words before they start school. Or perhaps your child is coming home from kindergarten anxious to apply their newfound word reading skills and you want to help them read even more words. The ability to read words comes over time and, like reading in general, is a process. How children learn to read was discussed in chapter 2; this chapter provides more information about how children learn to read or decode words.

Recall that children progress from knowing letters and letter sounds to putting those sounds together to sound out words. Then they create an understanding of that word using their knowledge of grammar and vocabulary. When they read the sentence "The cow nibbled on the flowers," they will combine their knowledge of a cow, what it means to nibble, and the type of flowers cows eat to create a mental image of a cow standing in a field eating clover. To get to this point, children progress through four phases in their ability to read words on the page (see the table below).[6]

Pre-alphabetic Phase

Children in this phase read words by remembering images or clues from the context the word is in.[7] For example, children use pictures that are around the word to recognize it. This is also when they recognize restaurant names and other words because of the context, or place that it is in. Without those cues—when the picture is removed or the restaurant name is written on a menu instead of on the sign outside—the child cannot read the word.

Overall, during this phase, children are more focused on what surrounds the word on the page or in the environment than on the letters and sounds that make up the word. During this phase, a child who has been read *The Cat in the Hat* by Dr. Seuss over and over will recite the words on the page and may use the pictures to remind them of what to say next. She may look at the picture to remember that the kids are flying a kite down the hall and on the end of the kite is mother's new dress.

Partial Alphabetic Phase

In the partial alphabetic phase, children know letter names, can read a few words on a page (without any context cues), and are learning that words are made up of sounds represented by letters.[8] In this phase, the child reading *The Cat in the Hat* can point to and sound out the letter sounds for small words, like *cat* and *hat*, and, as they learn, words like *fish* and *dish* that have more complex sound combinations ("sh" combines to say /shhh/).

Full Alphabetic Phase

In the full alphabetic phase, children have greater knowledge of letter sounds and how to decode or read words and can apply their knowledge of letter sounds to read words.[9] In this phase, they also remember words they have read in the past, building a bank of words that they can draw from to read quickly (remember the reading skill of fluency that was covered in chapter 2).[10] In kindergarten and first grade especially, explicit, systematic instruction, or instruction that provides kids with clear explanation and practice of letters in a planned order, is important to help children master skills.[11] This involves showing students different letter patterns and having them engage in lots of practice.

The full alphabetic phase involves reading full words and applying knowledge of word reading skills to words they have never read before.[12] When reading *The Cat in the Hat*, they may attempt to read longer words. Children understand and remember all the ways that sounds can be written, for example, that the long I sound (as in *rice*) can be written "igh" (*night*), "i" (*kite*), and "y" (*sky*) among other ways.

When children have full knowledge of the sounds in words they know, they can make connections between written and spoken words when they read a word in print for the first time. For example, a child who knows that the word *pig* has three phonemes will anticipate seeing three letters and the sounds /p/ /i/ and /g/ when they encounter the word *pig* in a story. This connection between expectation and reality helps children build memory for words, and when they read new words, they retain the entire words in their memories, creating a bank of words that they recognize "by sight" or just by looking.[13]

Consolidated Alphabetic Phase

In the final phase, the consolidated alphabetic phase, children read longer words because they notice patterns in words (-*ing*, -*ed*, -*tion*) and can chunk parts of words together.[14] For example, they would read the word *denominator* in chunks, as /de/ /nom/ /in/ /a/ /tor/, rather than as eleven separate sounds.

After children have learned to read words in chunks, they gain automaticity, or the ability to automatically recognize the meaning and pronunciation of words without expending energy or memory to decode them.[15] This is important because when children automatically recognize words, they can focus their effort during reading on understanding what they read, not on sounding out every word. This is also why it's important to continue to read picture books to your child even after they have started reading on their own. The books that young children start reading often have limited difficulty, and the words in them are simple, repeated words. Continuing Active Reading even after your child learns to read words on their own provides a balanced diet of practice with text they can decode on their own and rich conversation with storybooks that will challenge their vocabulary and thinking.

How Children Learn to Read Words

Phase	What happens in this phase?	What might I see in my reader?
Pre-alphabetic	• Children "read" through memory and by using the pictures. • Children are focused on the images or context that surrounds the word, not the letters in the word itself.	• The child repeats the story by saying sentences she has memorized from your read-aloud sessions. She looks at the pictures when she "reads." • A child recognizes a familiar restaurant name because of the sign's location.
Partial Alphabetic	• Children know letter names and sounds and can read a few words on the page without context clues.	• The child can read a word if you write it on a paper, with no picture cue.
Full Alphabetic	• Children are reading more and more words, including words they have never read before.	• The child can read different letter combinations and can read the words in text they have never seen before.
Consolidated Alphabetic	• Children notice longer spelling patterns (*-tion*, *-ing*). • Children are able to read more words quickly because their word recognition becomes automatic.	• The child's reading starts to sound more like an adult's reading.

The process that children go through to learn to read words is complex, and while the process is the same for each child, the age and speed of children's progress varies from child to child. Active Reading can support the learning process of all children by helping them learn to read words and see word patterns in context.

📖
What to Remember

• Children go through a process to learn how to read words. The process advances from knowing letter sounds to putting sounds together to reading words that are new to them.
• The goal of word reading is to read words automatically, without taking time to sound out each word. When children can read words automatically, they can focus on understanding what they read.
• Even when children learn how to read and are excited to practice with beginning reading books, engaging children in Active Reading with complex picture books helps them build their vocabulary and language.

FROM SINGING TO READING

As your preschooler walks into kindergarten, all the nursery rhymes, singing, and listing to rhyming words pay off as they use their ability to break
words into smaller parts (phonemic awareness) to read words on their own.
The practice of finding letters in books helps them as they use their letter
knowledge right away to start to figure out how to read new words. Finding
rhyming words in books, playing with language, and naming and talking about
letters during Active Reading are ways to reinforce important early skills in
young children. Throughout this book, we've mentioned books that are great
for Active Reading, and having access to books makes Active Reading possible and more likely. Chapter 8 explores how to build a home or classroom
library of books that are ideal for Active Reading.

· 8 ·

The Active Reading Bookshelf

Building a Library for Active Reading

*T*he books in three-year-old Jude's bedroom are piled in boxes, arranged on shelves with their covers easy to see, and stacked next to his bed. In a corner of the den, a child-sized armchair sits next to low shelves that have books displayed, covers facing out. His mother, a teacher, started Jude's library when he was an infant, and the board books that he chewed on (and read) as a baby are still in the boxes of books he sifted through as a toddler and now "reads" as a preschooler. It's easy to see how Jude could spend lots of time reading each day, and while having stacks and piles of books is not an absolute necessity, having some books for a child to call their own is important as they grow into readers.

Having books at home, however you get them—the local library, hand-me-downs, or gifts—is important. When kids have access to books, they're encouraged to read. Which books they have is important, too. When we do Active Reading, we're asking books to do a lot—teach print knowledge and concepts, teach new words, teach story structure, start a conversation—so we want the books our children read to do all that, with engaging illustrations and text that they can connect to. It's no small task!

Of course, you can engage your child in Active Reading using any book, especially when you think about getting your child to take over more and more of the storytelling. Still, as you start engaging your child in Active Reading, you'll find that some books are easier to talk about than others. Some books are more fun to spend time with. Those with interesting illustrations, characters your child can connect with, and scenarios that are relevant to your child's interest or experience are more likely to get read again and again. This chapter focuses on the importance of access to books for all kids and how to build libraries at home and in the classroom for Active Reading.

ACCESS TO BOOKS

It makes sense that having access to books, or being able to find, choose, and read a book when you want to, helps children become better readers.[1] For children, having books at home makes reading an everyday experience, something they can expect to engage with whenever they feel like reading or being read to. Of course, it's important for kids to have access to books in the places they spend most of their time—at home and in classrooms.

Books at Home

Having books at home, in tubs on the floor or on shelves that they can reach, teaches children that books are a part of growing up and a fun way to spend time. In fact, the number of books in a child's home is the one thing that correlates significantly with their reading scores.[2] Some researchers think that having books in the home creates a home culture that influences kids' academic performance, regardless of other factors (e.g., family income, parent's education level).[3] This influence could be as simple as keeping books at the front of kids' minds.

When books are on the floor and easily within reach of little hands, children will pick them up and engage with them in ways they can't if books are stored out of reach. Of course, access to books requires support from parents; when families reinforce the idea that reading is fun, by encouraging a child who toddles over with a book to read or asking relatives to give books as gifts, children are more motivated to read and interested in reading as a desirable activity.[4]

This is important because not all children have access to books. And a lack of books has a meaningful impact on kids' readiness to learn to read. Children in homes that have fewer books are less able to recognize their letters or to mimic the behavior of reading a book.[5] However, children do not need shelves stacked full of books to get this benefit, and they don't have to own many books either.

Children who have access to books at home, at school, and in their public library have higher reading scores than those who do not.[6] Books are one of the few things of which we can decisively say "more is better." Fourth-grade students in the United States who report reading frequently each week and have one hundred or more books at home on average (think about having an entire bookshelf full of books) are proficient readers.[7]

American fourth graders who report enjoying reading but don't have plenty of books at home fall short of this benchmark. Yet a third of American fourth graders report having no more than a single bookshelf of books of any kind at home.[8] More than giving kids something to do, having five hundred books in the home compared to no books confers the same increased impact on children's reading achievement as having a parent who earned a university degree rather than one who dropped out of high school.[9] Books matter.

Books at School

For some children who do not have enough books at home, being able to read books at school is an important part of their day. One study found that the ratio of books to children in middle-income neighborhoods was thirteen to one, meaning that there were thirteen books for every one child in that area. In the same city, there was *only one book for every three hundred children* in low-income neighborhoods.[10] This means that having access to books in common spaces like schools and libraries is especially important for young children growing up in lower-income neighborhoods. Programs like Dolly Parton Imagination Library and Raising a Reader focus on addressing this challenge. (See appendix C for more suggestions.)

Providing books in schools and daycare centers can help address this problem. In one study, three- and four-year-old classrooms in child-care centers were given more than three hundred books and classrooms were made into literacy-rich zones. When this happened, children became more engaged with books, meaning that they picked up books and read them more often. They were also more excited about the books. Furthermore, students who were involved in the classrooms that received the books scored higher on important kindergarten reading skills (letter knowledge, rhyming, alliteration, concepts of writing).[11] The take-away from this study is that providing books and allowing children time to explore them is a valuable use of time.

What to Remember

- Having children's books at home and in early childhood classrooms is important for all children. Having books that are available for children to read when they want makes reading a fun activity that children will choose.
- Not all children have access to books, but it doesn't take a lot of books to make a difference. When children have at least one shelf's worth of books (twenty-five titles) to call their own, it is enough to make a difference on their later reading success.
- The more books kids have at home and school, the better. When a child has access to more books as they learn how to read, it promotes reading achievement and increases their odds of later success.

HOW TO BUILD AN ACTIVE READING LIBRARY

Books are important, but so is the budget. So what is the best way to build a home or classroom library that keeps a child's interest over time? The important thing to consider is matching the books to the child's age level in terms of length, concepts, and theme. Above all, books should be appealing to children. These are the books that become favorites and are read over and over, increasing the amount that kids learn from them. For a start, look to the classics. There are some popular titles that have withstood the test of time (see the table below) with a combination of strong illustrations; clear stories; engaging, relatable characters; and fun-to-read text (more book suggestions are included in appendix A).

Classic Active Reading Books

Title	Author	What Makes This an Active Reading Classic
Where the Wild Things Are	Maurice Sendak	A relatable character in Max and a clear connection to the feelings that young children have when they get in trouble.
The Snowy Day	Ezra Jack Keats	The everyday story of a boy playing in the snow captured in bright illustrations.
Corduroy	Don Freeman	A lovable bear discovering his world for the first time in a story with a clear problem, solution, and message about friendship.
The Very Hungry Caterpillar	Eric Carle	A story with real-life information about caterpillars and butterflies in a story that young children can follow easily.
The Runaway Bunny	Margaret Wise Brown	A little bunny threatening to run away from home with fun illustrations that young children can both relate to and ponder.
The Little Engine That Could	Watty Piper	A story with a repeatable chorus that every young child can fill-in-the-blank and then apply to their own life: I think I can . . .
Harry the Dirty Dog	Gene Zion	The story of a dog who is naughty but still loved by his family has a clear story arc with lots to talk about in the illustrations.

Choosing Books for Active Reading

The ABCs of Active Reading can be done with any book. However, some books lend themselves better to Active Reading than others. A book's quality (story and illustrations) impacts just how much you can talk about the characters, pictures, and story.[12] That's important because, as you'll recall, you're reading these books over and over again! Books with more depth are those that you can ask story questions and open-ended questions about (chapter 4), that have rich vocabulary, and that are relevant to kids' lives or that spark a new interest.

There are five aspects of books that contribute to their complexity or depth when it comes to creating a conversation with your child: theme, character development, illustration, language, and plot.

Theme

Theme is the idea that a book communicates either explicitly through a stated message or implicitly through the characters, plot, and dialogue. For children, theme is an aspect of the book that they will connect to. For example, the theme of the *Corduroy* books by Don Freeman is friendship as shown by the experiences of Lisa and her best friend, the bear Corduroy. Your child may connect with this theme simply by appreciating that Corduroy has found a friend in Lisa.

The theme of the book *Mama, Do You Love Me?* by Barbara Joosse is unconditional parental love, and your child may connect with the theme by talking about how you show love in your family. Talking about the theme of books is important to develop children's understanding of stories as more than just a series of events but as a way to connect with books, learn new information, and think through life lessons.[13]

It is important to note, however, that some books do not have broad themes but can just be a fun story to read. *Good Night, Gorilla* by Peggy Rathmann, *The Napping House* by Audrey and Don Wood, and *Jamberry* by Bruce Degen are all books that do not have clear themes but nonetheless are fun to read and talk about.

Characters

Characters in picture books are often one-dimensional or "flat." This means that they tend to make the same choices no matter what. Think about Corduroy making the same basic observation and mischief in each of the *Corduroy* books. Or Curious George having the same basic story (he's curious, he does something he shouldn't, he's rescued, everyone forgives him because something good comes out of it). This lack of depth is just fine for young children who are connecting with storybook characters at a basic level.

This level of character is also good for young children because they present a clear example of how something in the world works that children can understand before they encounter more complex characters. They also allow young children to talk about characters in a concrete way. For example, a child may use their knowledge of Curious George, who is always curious, to predict what George will do next in a story they are reading for the first time. Finally, characters that are familiar enough for young children to understand help them connect and think about how we have traits that may not change (Curious George will always be curious).

In comparison to "flat" characters whose responses do not change regardless of what happens to them, "round characters" are similar to kids—they are changing and dynamic.[14] Round characters may act one way in one situation and another way in another situation.

In picture books, we see this when characters change from the start of a story to the end (though round characters are more common in chapter books and texts that children will read later). For example, in *Julius, the Baby of the World* by Kevin Henkes, new big sister Lilly hates her baby brother, Julius, until she has to defend him. This simple change shows how we can have experiences that force a shift in our feelings, in this case from despising to protecting a new sibling. Having round characters in stories encourages kids to talk about how people change, what causes change, and how we can connect our lives to those of the characters in books.

Twenty years ago, 9 percent of characters in children's books were diverse, meaning that they represented a nonwhite experience. In 2016, that percent had more than doubled to 22 percent but was still below the percent of our population that is diverse.[15] All children should read stories that feature children from nonmajority backgrounds experiencing everything from a snow day (*The Snowy Day* by Ezra Jack Keats) to visiting a library (*Lola at the Library* by Anna McQuinn).

Regardless of the race or ethnicity of your child, you can use books to give them a head start to understand the diversity they will see in the broader world. Children should have healthy book diets with characters and situations that "mirror" their own lives and experiences, as well as books that provide "windows" into the lives of people and communities different than their own. Books with diverse characters provide for the opportunity to talk about how our experiences are different and similar and what we can learn from each other. (See appendix A for a list of diverse books that are great for Active Reading.)

Plot

Events, or the plot, are the heart of any story. In picture books, a plot often revolves around a problem and solution. An engaging plot intrigues readers and provides lots of opportunities for them to talk about and think about what happened and why. Children will wonder what happens next and how the problem is going to get resolved. Young children typically do best with plots that are connected to their own experiences.[16]

Stories that are good for young children have clear accounts of connected events that tell a simple sequence. For example, in the story *Lola at the Library* by Anna McQuinn and illustrated by Rosalind Beardshaw, pictures of Lola preparing to go and going to the library provide context for this simple story. They also provide an example of an African American character engaged in a familiar experience, encouraging children of all backgrounds to make connections. Beardshaw spent time thinking through the details on each page, carrying items from page to page, encouraging children to notice how Lola uses a backpack, for example, at home and then at the library. This story is a short sequence of events that children can relate to and talk about.

Similarly, in *Corduroy* by Don Freeman, the problem is clear—Corduroy, the bear, has lost his button and must find it. Corduroy tries to find it by exploring the department store that he lives in, discovering mattresses, a night guard, and more along the way. This simple story allows children to talk about what Corduroy wants and how he goes about getting it. It also provides them the opportunity to think about the story from other perspectives. What does Lisa, the little girl, want? What does the night watchman think?

In picture books with plot events, as children read them, they can also think about the sequence of the story and talk about what happens first, second, next, and last. Conversations about story sequence help children organize information they find in books and build an understanding of story structure, or how stories are organized.

Illustration

Book illustrations are an important element for Active Reading. It is important for books to have strong illustrations that children can engage with. Pictures help children define words, understand the story, and extend their understanding by providing information that they can use to make inferences and predictions.

Books with strong illustrations combine words and images so that the two are more effective at telling the story than either on its own. The picture would not mean as much without the words and the words would not tell the full story without the pictures. When we combine an understanding of words and pictures, we are building comprehension through both, something even young children can do.[17]

In the book *What Daddies Like* by Judy Nevin and illustrated by Stephanie Six, the illustrations provide a clear picture of what the baby bear and his daddy are doing, as well as smaller subplots within each page. In the book *Good Night, Gorilla* by Peggy Rathmann, the main story is of a gorilla sneaking out of the zoo and taking his animal friends with him, but children can talk about any number of details in the pictures, including where the mouse holding the banana is on each page and how the mouse relates to the gorilla. It's details like these that make illustrations a wonderful way to build language.

Language

We have already talked about the language in picture books as it relates to vocabulary (chapter 5); however, it is worth revisiting the importance of language in general. Books with strong language have more than rhyming or flowery language; they have well-crafted sentences that communicate a story and leave room for discussion.[18] Each word is chosen and each sentence is carefully written to make each phrase count.[19] Books like the Bear series by Karma Wilson (*Bear Snores On*, *Bear Says Thanks*, and others) are great examples of how authors use language to engage kids in stories that kids can "read" along with (fill-in-the-blank), connect to, and talk about.

There are two aspects of the words in books that are important considerations for Active Reading: repetitive text and Rare Words.

Repetitive text encourages kids to engage with the book through fill-in-the-blank prompts (chapter 3), while rhyming books reinforce phonemic awareness (chapter 7). Think about the repeated text in *The Little Engine That Could* by Watty Piper. Even as an adult, you can probably chug chug along with the little blue engine as she puffs merrily up the hill chanting: I think I can, I think I can. *The Napping House* by Don and Audrey Wood presents a repeated chant for children to complete as each character falls into and wakes up from their nap. And you may have grown up on the rhyming books of Dr. Seuss, books that are best for helping kids hear the similarities and differences in words in the stories of *The Cat in the Hat* and *Green Eggs and Ham*.

Books that are good for Active Reading include lots of interesting or Rare Words. Rare Words are those that are important for the story and that add meaning and imagery for the reader (Rare Words are covered in depth in chapter 5).

Aspects of Books

Aspect	Definition	Book Examples
Theme	The idea in a text that is communicated through the story and characters. The lesson or take-away from a story.	*Corduroy* by Don Freeman *Mama, Do You Love Me?* by Barbara Joosse
Characters	Characters that are either flat (predictable) or round (dynamic). Also characters that present a variety of experiences and character backgrounds.	*Curious George* by H. A. Rey (flat) *Julius, the Baby of the World* by Kevin Henkes (round) *Lola at the Library* by Anna McQuinn (diverse) *The Snowy Day* by Ezra Jack Keats (diverse)
Illustrations	The illustrations are complex and support and expand the story. The pictures and words work together to tell the story.	*What Daddies Like* by Judy Nevin *Good Night, Gorilla* by Peggy Rathmann
Language	Language that is crafted by the author to communicate the story; not too many or too few words. Language that provides repetition and Rare Words encourage Active Reading.	*Bear Snores On* by Karma Wilson *The Napping House* by Don and Audrey Wood
Plot	A story that is interesting and that makes sense; a plot that makes the reader want to know what happens next and with events that tie together.	*Corduroy* by Don Freeman *Lola at the Library* by Anna McQuinn

Some books are better at different aspects than others (see Aspects of Books table). When you choose books for Active Reading, it's not important that every book has characters that your child immediately connects to, wonderful rhythmic language with many Rare Words, a complex plot, and a complex theme. Instead, seek out books that are great at a few aspects of Active Reading and look to add new books that contribute something different to your child's reading "diet." In the Sample Active Reading Library table, you can see that not every book has all the aspects that are great for Active Reading, so it is helpful when children can focus in on what makes a book really special, talking about what happens to Max and Ruby in *Bunny Cakes*, for example, or connecting their experience of getting a new baby brother to Dot in *Wolfie the Bunny* by Ame Dyckman.

Sample Active Reading Library

Book	Illustration	Story	Characters	Language	Rare Words
Sheep in a Jeep by Nancy Shaw				X	X
Bunny Cakes by Rosemary Wells	X	X	X		X
Beekle: The Unimaginary Friend by Dan Santat	X	X	X		X
Owl Babies by Martin Waddell		X	X		X
Wolfie the Bunny by Ame Dyckman	X	X	X		X
Llama Llama Red Pajama by Anna Dewdney		X	X	X	
Mr. Tiger Goes Wild by Peter Brown	X	X	X		X

What to Remember

• When building a home library, consider matching books with a child's age level in the length of book they can listen to, the concepts in the book, and what the book is about.

• The ultimate goal of a home or classroom library is to have books that are appealing to children.

• For Active Reading, we want books that can produce interesting conversations. Consider a book's illustrations, plot, characters, and theme when choosing a book that will be good for Active Reading.

• Children should have opportunities to see themselves in books, reading books with characters that have similar backgrounds and experiences as them, as well as the opportunity to see other experiences in books with characters and experiences different than their own.

• Also, look for books that have strong language and Rare Words and that are fun to read.

ACTIVE READING AND INFORMATIONAL TEXT

Saha sits in a cardboard box, marker in hand. She draws a circle along one wall of the box, buttons on the other, and a rectangle in the center. "I'm in a truck," she says, "and this is an outrigger."

Saha learned about outriggers (parts of large trucks that extend out and help the truck keep its balance when lifting heavy loads) from *The Big Book of Big Trucks* (Usborne). For weeks, she pored over the trucks book: monster trucks, cherry pickers, and rocket movers. She learned content-specific words, like *boom* and *outrigger*. She pointed at different-colored booms on the trucks and described what the people in pictures were doing ("He's covering his ears because the trucks are so loud") and describing parts of each truck ("the cab is at the top of the ladder on this truck"). Finally, she incorporated her knowledge of trucks into pretend play, turning a cardboard box into her own big truck.

This kind of knowledge about a topic, in this case trucks, is built from and enhanced by Active Reading. Books that support content knowledge, like informational texts (or nonfiction), that are great for Active Reading have the same qualities as narrative texts that are good for Active Reading: good illustrations, clear language, content-specific vocabulary (appendix A). Finding great informational books for Active Reading means finding books about a topic that your child is interested in that include strong pictures that can help them understand factual information and build background knowledge (chapter 6).

What to Remember

- Informational text, or nonfiction books, are wonderful for helping children build knowledge about a topic.
- The aspects that make children's nonfiction good are the same ones that make fiction books great—illustration, clear language, rich vocabulary.
- To find good informational text for Active Reading, start with what the child is interested in, then find books that provide for a strong conversation about that topic.

THE ACTIVE READING BOOKSHELF

Building a library is not about having every single book you can buy, and finding a good book for Active Reading doesn't mean finding a book that has all the aspects of great literature—detailed illustrations, Rare Words, relatable characters, poetic language—all at once. We want kids to have exposure to lots of different books, some that do illustrations best, some that have language that is fun to read over and over, and some with characters that resonate. As children grow their experience with Active Reading, it's time to put it all together. In chapter 9, we will conclude with an overview of how parents have engaged their children in Active Reading as well as responses to common questions about Active Reading.

· 9 ·

Time to Read

Doing Active Reading

I sat with my daughters, Saha, three, and Neina, two, at the kitchen table. Reading books during snack and sometimes mealtimes (when the whole family wasn't sitting down together) had become a routine as we tried to squeeze in as much reading as possible during weekdays that were already busy with work, daycare, and toddler schedules. I wanted to get in as many books as possible and had resorted to reading for ten to fifteen minutes while they ate a snack. I opened the book *Rosie's Hat* by Julia Donaldson. Saha had read the book before, but it was Neina's first time.

"What's happening on this page?" I asked on the first page where a little girl held on to her hat while standing in a field overlooking a cliff.

"Rosie's holding on to her hat," Saha said, mid-bite.

"The hat!" Neina exclaimed, pointing to the picture of the hat.

"That's right!" I said. "Rosie's holding on to her hat. Let's see what happens." I turned the page.

"The hat blew away," Neina exclaimed, leaning over to point at the hat, now in the distance.

"The hat did blow away, and what is Rosie doing?" I asked.

Neina looked at the picture.

"She's crying," said Saha.

"She is crying. Rosie's crying because her hat blew away. Where do you think it's going to go?"

"In the air," said Neina.

"It is in the air. Let's see what happens."

We continued through the book like that, commenting on each page, each girl contributing. For Saha, who had read the book before, sometimes the contributions were in response to questions that she was learning how

111

to answer (Why is Rosie crying?) and that she wasn't able to answer the first time we'd read *Rosie's Hat*, when she was Neina's age. For Neina, experiencing the book for the first time, her responses were genuine surprise or amusement at all the places the hat ended up. Saha soon tired of *Rosie's Hat*, but Neina and I read it over and over in the coming weeks. Neina learned how to retell the story, just as Saha had.

*P*arenting and working with young children comes with a long list of to-dos: fulfilling requests for more cereal or strawberries cut just right, hours of playing on the floor with blocks and puzzles, taking the kids outside to let off steam, not to mention naptime and the other household errands that have to happen each day. At the end of the day, it's easy to look back and wonder if Active Reading happened or if it happened well. Did the three books before nap count as Active Reading? Is that enough to make a difference? We hope by now you know that Active Reading is something that, even when done in small doses, one book at a time or five minutes in between building block towers, can have a big impact on your child's language and early literacy skills.

Parents who shift from reading *to* their kids to reading *with* them say that when they make the change to Active Reading, they find themselves reading more with their children without planning to. Perhaps their child brings them more books to read, or they carve out more time during the day for an activity that both they and their child look forward to and find valuable. That's not to say it's easy—nothing in parenting ever is, especially at first—but reminding yourself to **A**sk Questions, **B**uild Vocabulary, and **C**onnect to your child's world will, over time, become not just Active Reading but the natural way you talk and read together.

This book has covered early literacy skills (print knowledge and print concepts; chapters 2 and 3), the ABCs of Active Reading (chapters 4, 5, and 6), phonemic awareness and letter knowledge phonics skills (chapter 7), and how to build a library for Active Reading (chapter 8). This chapter ends the book with more ways to tackle some of the challenges that may come up (for example, reading with kids who are two different ages), the current conversation around e-readers and e-books (is e-reading still Active Reading?), and how to build a joy and love of reading in your child.

ONE BOOK AT A TIME: ANSWERING QUESTIONS
ABOUT ACTIVE READING

At this point, you may have questions about Active Reading that we haven't addressed. We've compiled questions that parents have asked and responses from parents who have handled each.

How do I know I'm doing Active Reading "right"?

You'll know you're doing it "right" when you read a book without doing the ABCs and notice that something is missing. Practice the ABCs of Active Reading and eventually they will become habit. You'll be thinking about questions you can ask on each page, looking for new words to talk about, and thinking of ways to connect what you're reading with your child's world.

There is no official script for how to do Active Reading (though appendix B does have book guides to give you ideas), so listen to how you and your child are engaging with the book. When you hear yourself stopping and talking about the story, listening for your child to respond, and, over time, listening to your child talk more and more each time you read a book, you're doing it right!

I'm doing Active Reading. What changes should I see in my child?

When she started Active Reading with her son, Monica McMahon noticed that she heard him using the illustrations to make predictions about what was going to happen in the story. You may notice your child using more words while you read, demanding to "read" the story to you, and eventually asking you questions or stopping you to interject their ideas and opinions. This is good! It shows you that they're thinking while you read and know that reading is a time to engage in conversation, not just sit back and listen (at least, not all the time).

Active Reading helps build young children's language and early literacy skills, so be on the lookout for how your child is using language as well as how they are using books. They may ask about the author or illustrator or connect two books by the same illustrator by noticing similarities in the pictures. When they read on their own, they may pick up a book and start "reading" or retelling the story to themselves with more complete sentences and ideas than they did before.

When you're running errands, you may hear them connect what they're seeing outside the car windows or at the park with what they just read. And when you are asking them questions as you read, you'll hear them giving longer and longer responses. Active Reading may tune you in to these broader changes that are happening beneath the surface even as you notice specific ones—your child using the word "vines" after you talk about it when reading *Madeline* by Ludwig Bemelmans, for example.

In addition to the changes in your child's language and literacy skills and abilities, you may also find your child asking to read more often during play time as reading becomes a favorite activity. You might notice your child pretending to read as they play on their own or with others. And you may notice that their expectations for what happens during reading time with you start to change. For example, instead of just waiting for you to turn the page, they may expect to answer questions, ask questions themselves, or try to direct the reading—telling you when they don't want to answer questions and they just want to hear the story or taking over the reading themselves.

How do you find time to do Active Reading?
There just doesn't seem to be enough time in the day!

First, Active Reading should not be a lesson or a set time of day. And as little as fifteen minutes, three times a week can make a big difference. In early childhood classrooms, noticing when children choose a book and, if you can, sitting with them to read it or planning to read to small groups of children throughout the day can make that difference. That said, we all want our kids to have more Active Reading and here are some ways that busy parents make that happen.

• **Three books at bedtime, a bin on Saturdays, and access to books in the car.** McMahon builds Active Reading into her bedtime routine. She and her son read three books before bed each weekday. On Saturdays, when there are longer stretches of time, she grabs a bin of books from the library and she and her three-year-old son cuddle up for about an hour in her bed. The bin of books then goes into the car for the week so her son can read them on the way to and from daycare each day. It's a special treat to read in Mom's bed on Saturdays, and McMahon uses Active Reading to preview the books he'll "read" on the way to and from school that week.

• **Don't skip the bedtime reading routine.** Sarah McNeill, nonprofit professional and mother of two in Charlotte, North Carolina, makes reading a must-do in the bedtime routine, even if it means staying up a little later. Her four-year-old reads four books each night—they read three books after bath and the fourth after teeth are brushed. "If we are running late, then we might choose shorter books or not go as deep with the ABCs," says McNeill, "but we don't skip reading."

• Similarly, Amanda Wilkinson, mother of two boys in Charlotte, also maintains a bedtime reading routine to make sure that they read every day. That is her biggest challenge though; the majority of weekday reading happens at bedtime, and at that point Wilkinson's primary focus is getting everyone to sleep. In retrospect, she says, she might have started a routine of one book that she does Active Reading with rather than three books that she may not take as much time with because of bedtime. If her son expected one book, she says, "Active Reading would feel like an easier lift at night."

• **Use books as an ever-ready distraction.** Wilkinson also keeps a basket of books in the living room and, when her four-year-old nags her for TV time, suggests reading instead. "I can usually suggest reading a book instead and he's just as excited," she says.

Making reading part of your daily routine and keeping books in spaces that you know you'll be (the living room, the car) will make it more likely that your child will spend time reading each day.

How do you read with two (or more) kids of different ages?
My preschooler wants to read, but my toddler can't sit still!

Wilkinson's boys are two and four years old, and it's inevitable that if the four-year-old wants to read, the two-year-old will too. So Wilkinson tries to pick books that will appeal to both her boys. Titles like *If You Give a Moose a Muffin* by Laura Numeroff, the Bear series (*Bear Snores On, Bear Says Thanks*) by Karma Wilson, and *The Pout Pout Fish* books by Deborah Diesen are all titles that both her boys enjoy.

She also picks out books from the library every two to three weeks so there are always new stories to choose from. Her four-year-old is more excited to read new stories than the ones he's seen around the house for years, and his little brother is happy to join in on any book. Still, Wilkinson has noticed a difference in how her boys read and she engages them in different ways.

Wilkinson's two-year-old has just graduated from board books to picture books. He likes to point at everything in the pictures, asking, "What's that?" This can get annoying but also forces Wilkinson to explain the story and label pictures before reading. With her four-year-old, Wilkinson gauges her son's mood and how familiar he is with the book they are reading. Her son talks more about the book when it is a book he's read before, but on the first reading, he doesn't like to be asked questions. Wilkinson will read the book without stopping the first time because her son wants to know what's going to happen next before she asks questions.

Wilkinson also models or shows her older son how to answer the questions she asks by answering them herself. She may ask, "How do you think Farmer Brown feels?" and then answer the question herself ("Hm, I'm looking at his face; he doesn't look happy to me"). After Wilkinson has shown her son how to answer the question, he's more likely to provide his own answers.

During bedtime reading, each boy brings two books to read. Wilkinson admits that the two-year-old tends to run around the room while the four-year-old listens, and if they're both listening to the same book, she may simplify the story by shortening the words she reads or talking more about the pictures instead of reading every word to keep both boys engaged. "I have found the bonding experience [of being read to together] to be really powerful," says Wilkinson. "They do a lot of laughing together and sometimes my four-year-old will point out things to his younger brother in the pictures."

Active Reading is less about reading each book perfectly with the ABCs and more about using the ABCs when your child or children are engaged in the story. Don't worry about the toddler who seems to refuse to cooperate when your older child is ready to listen; eventually the toddler will grow into the preschooler who's (finally) ready to sit.

There are some chapter books that I can't wait to read with my child.
When and how should we start my child on chapter books?
Can I do the ABCs with a chapter book?

You can do the ABCs with a chapter book, though you'll be talking about the text more than the pictures. McNeill's older daughter is starting to enjoy short picture books, like the *Princess in Black* books by Shannon Hale and the *Mercy Watson* series by Kate DiCamillo. These books have some pictures that children can use as reference points but also have longer stories that help them learn how longer books unfold.

When you do the ABCs with a chapter book, focus on asking a few questions every chapter that help you know whether your child is following the story. Pick out vocabulary words that are important for understanding the story. Ideally, you'll see those words multiple times throughout the book.

You can also encourage your child to stop and ask you when they hear a word they don't know. That way you know you're building their vocabulary at just the right points in the story. Make connections to your child's world and other books he or she may have read. Also, when you start a new chapter, ask your child what has happened in the story so far. When you do that, you're helping them summarize and keep up with the story's thread.

One major difference between reading chapter books and picture books is that you probably won't read a chapter book together more than once, so a major focus, as you shift to chapter books, is on enjoying the story and the experience of reading together.

I've tried and tried, but my kid won't sit still to do Active Reading.
What do I do?

First, you're not alone. Kids are active and, especially as children develop language, doing the language work in Active Reading may be difficult for some children. Or they may just want to play. Keep books available and at kid level so they can choose books if they want. Then try to follow their lead as much as possible.

If they choose a book, talk about the pictures before you launch into the story to see if a picture walk would help your child engage with the book in a new way. Even if you only get through a few pictures, that's a start! Also, look for books that connect to their interests, with stories or information that they can connect to their favorite toys or games. Does your child love trucks, diggers, and all things with wheels? Fill his bookshelf with books that will teach him all about his favorite trucks. Then, as you read, ask connection questions (Do you have a dump truck? What did you do with your dump truck?). This will make reading relevant to his life right now and give him information that he can transfer to play.

My child has special needs. Is Active Reading something that will "work" for her?

The short answer: yes! Jim Trelease, author of *The Read Aloud Handbook*, describes the powerful impact that reading aloud can have on young children with special needs. Active Reading techniques have been found to be effective with children who are what researchers call "at risk," meaning that they may have a developmental delay.[1] They have also been successful with young children who are deaf or hard-of-hearing.[2] And children with disabilities have shown gains in vocabulary from Active Reading techniques.[3] All children benefit from time spent reading, and the focus of engaging children on their level is one that seeks out children's strengths.

Language and learning vocabulary words are skills that most children can develop, even if they do so at their own pace. As a parent, you know what your child's strengths and interests are and can draw them out through the books you choose and the ABC opportunities you provide while reading to your child.

*We don't speak English at home. Can Active Reading in my native language
help my child when she attends an English-speaking school?*

Yes. Active Reading can be done in any language, and the process and outcomes are the same. For example, in one study, children who speak a language
other than English at home have been taught using Active Reading strategies
(dialogic reading) in Spanish (their native language) and showed growth in
both English and Spanish.[4] In fact, when children have a strong grasp of one
language, it transfers to a second language when they learn to read.[5] You
can be confident that using Active Reading to strengthen your child's native
language will support their language development as they learn English in the
school setting.

IS E-READING ACTIVE READING?

There are the official recommendations (for children ages two to five, limit
screens to one hour per day of high-quality programming, ideally with you
playing or watching with them[6]) and then there is reality (the need to engage
your child in something while you finish dinner, even though they already
watched an hour of cartoons that morning). However you try to structure
your day, tablets and e-readers are a fact of life for young children. Accord-
ing to Common Sense Media, 61 percent of lower-income families and 85
percent of higher-income families have some kind of tablet.[7] And there's no
debate that they capture kids' attention.

The jury is out on whether e-readers benefit young children in terms
of their reading skills and, if they benefit, how much. Thinking about Active Reading, the question is not whether to expose your child to a tablet or
screen at all, but what parents should know about e-reading as a way to build
kids' early language and literacy skills. This section isn't about the debate but
what to know and how to make your child's time with e-readers (tablets and
e-books, not apps or games) beneficial.

The Benefit Your Child Gets May Depend on Age

Your child simply may not be able to gain as much from reading an e-book
when they are a young toddler (younger than two years) compared to when
they are older (two years and up). When it comes to generalizing words, or
learning words that they can use in other contexts, from books, young toddlers
may need traditional books, while older toddlers and preschoolers can learn
from e-books as well.[8]

Similarly, kindergarteners who had low language skills invested more effort when reading e-books with animation, perhaps because the animation maintained their interest.[9] All this together, when you choose e-books for your child, think about how old they are and what you want them to gain from the reading experience. As your child gets older, they can learn more from e-books, though the ABCs and print books are still important.

Focus on the Story

The current research suggests that children's comprehension of storybooks is lower when they are read e-books, and they appear to do less talking about what they read when they read on tablets.[10] This may be because of how adults are talking with kids while reading e-books. When parents read e-books with bells and whistles, they tend to talk about what the e-book can do (What happens when you press the hippo? What does this button do?) rather than the story itself. Take advantage of repeated readings to make sure you're talking more about the story than the buttons, games, and animation.[11]

Don't Forget to Point

When reading e-books, research shows that parents are less likely to point at objects when describing them.[12] Nonverbal cues like pointing are important to help children learn new words and maintain their focus on the book.

Look for Simple e-Books

When parents read simple e-books to young toddlers (under age two), research shows they engage in the same level of parent-talk compared to when they read print books. However, they read the words less, which may be due to the narration feature on the e-books.[13] Don't let the e-book take over features that are important for you and your child to experience together with Active Reading, like engaging with the words on the page and having your child tell you what's happening. Choosing e-books that do not turn into games may be one way to maximize an e-library for your Active Reading at home.

More Animations and Sound Effects, Fewer Games and Hotspots

Today's e-books are much different than the original CD-ROM computer books. Books today often have animation (tap on the animals to see the animals stampede) or even games built into the books. Some features, like animations and sound effects, support kids' learning, while others (games and hotspots) distract kids from the purpose or learning in the book.[14] Children labeled more pictures when their hotspot access, or ability to click on animations or other in-app features, was limited in an e-book, compared to when there were no restrictions.[15] Look for books that allow you to disable games and other distractions so you can maximize how your child engages with the story.

Apply the ABCs of Active Reading

Just like pointing, **A**sking questions, **B**uilding vocabulary, and **C**onnecting to the child's world are important parts of reading e-books or "tree books" (paper books). Just like when you are reading a picture book and may stop on every page to ask a question or talk about what's happening, do the same thing with e-books. Ask your child what is happening in the story, and talk about Rare Words you find (chapter 5). E-books may even have animations that show you what the word means; the hippopotamus may hide behind a tree to show the word "shy" or a bunch of animals may run together to show "stampede." When you can, use the e-book to make your talk about the book richer.

Use Screen Time to Build Background Knowledge and Encourage Learning

Background knowledge becomes increasingly important as children become independent readers (chapter 6). Using apps and media to teach children about things that interest them is a great way to use screens to advance kids' knowledge and later reading skill. If your child is interested in something, use their tablet to explore the topic through videos, books, and more.

All Screen Time Is Not the Same

It's important to diversify kids' experiences so that they have a blend of traditional and e-book experiences. Compared to paper "tree books," the research so far appears to suggest that kids learn less from screens, even when they are used to watching screens at home much of the time.[16] For now, when it comes to building your children's language and literacy skills, it does seem that less passive screen time is better,[17] and your child e-reading by themselves is no substitute for e-reading with you (or another caring adult).

RAISING KIDS WHO LOVE TO READ

At the start of this book, we imagined the child who loves to read—the child who refuses to put down a book and breaks rules to finish a chapter. We want our children to love reading, and Active Reading is one way to encourage children to love stories through their interactions with the adults in their lives.[18] We know it's important to show kids that adults read, and the best way to do that is to open a novel ourselves. But, honestly, after everything that has to get done in a day, not to mention the attention that young kids require, modeling reading by sitting down in an armchair yourself might not be an option. Or perhaps you don't love reading yourself and have trouble getting through even the latest page-turner. That's okay. Here are a few ideas to create spaces that will help children grow up to be lifelong lovers of books.

Give Your Child a Choice

As adults, we gravitate toward our favorite type of books and avoid things we don't want to read (even if we eventually have to read our taxes, a technical manual, or a work report). Knowing what we like to read and how to choose books is an important skill for kids to learn. We can start this early by providing kids with choices in what they choose for read aloud and what they choose to read as they start to read on their own. Giving kids a choice may look like providing a few picture books and asking a child what they want to read first before you start reading together or letting them choose the three books they read before bed, regardless of how many times you've read that book already that day.

Make Books Available

Similarly, having books available, in bins on the floor, on low shelves, even in piles, makes it more likely that kids will choose books when they're playing (chapter 8). When a child flits from toy to toy, books are likely to be one of the things they naturally choose if books are in their play space. It goes without saying that young children's books are consumable items and, when they are loved, will become dirty, ripped, and even destroyed. Find ways to add books to your child's library (like the Dolly Parton Imagination Library, library sales, or having a book-themed birthday party to get more titles) so that you aren't worried about the inevitable wear and tear.

Create a Cozy Reading Space

Once books are available and your child has chosen what he wants, creating an inviting space to read could be as simple as hanging a blanket over two chairs to create a reading cave. Let your child bring their bedtime blanket to the couch for reading time to make it cozier. Or fill a chair with stuffed animals when it is reading time. Pinterest is full of book nook ideas complete with themes and Do-It-Yourself projects, but for a child, an inviting space may be the one that they create themselves from their own favorite blankets, stuffed animals, and books.

Follow Your Child's Interests

Your child will start developing interests—perhaps she starts ballet lessons and is curious about dancing, or maybe he's seen a TV show about lions and had questions that lasted long after the credits rolled. When your child has questions about something or expresses interest about a topic, that could be your cue to visit the local library. It's also a potential opportunity to help him build background knowledge that will prepare him for school (see chapter 6 for more on the importance of background knowledge). Visit your local library and ask the librarians for help to find books about the topic.

Think beyond Books

Reading is reading is reading. Exposing your child to things that we can read for fun (magazines), to learn how to do something (cookbooks), and to find out answers to questions (a TV guide) shows them how useful reading is. In particular, magazines for young children can provide an inexpensive way to increase the amount of text that your child has access to while building a love of a new topic. Magazines like *Highlights High Five* and *Ladybug* have stories and poems. *Ranger Rick Junior* and *National Geographic Kids* are all about animals.

Get Creative

Monica McMahon gives her four-year-old a headlamp to read with before he goes to bed at night. Local libraries host Paws to Read events that pair kids with a dog to read with. Encourage your child to read to their stuffed animal buddies, seek out a new event at a public library, or give them a flashlight or magnifying glass to "read" with. Any time that you capitalize on young children's sense of fun and novelty, you're making reading something unexpected and fun.

READ WITH ME

Academically, for researchers, it's easy to get excited about Active Reading. Few interventions have been so well studied and produced positive results so consistently. But, as parents, Active Reading is less about research and more about seeing bedtime, story time, or Saturday cuddle time become the most powerful time in your child's day. In Charlotte, North Carolina, where we live and work, we have seen parents connect with the ABCs of Active Reading, use them well, and see changes in their children right away. It's a small change—reading *with* a child instead of *to* them—and it doesn't take a lot of time (fifteen-minute sessions, three times a week[19]), but it makes all the difference in the world.

Appendix A

Books for Active Reading

It's impossible to list every book that would be great for Active Reading, but here is a list that you can use to start or grow a child's library. If you find an author or illustrator you love or character that you really like reading about, let that inspire you to find even more titles for Active Reading.

GREAT BOOKS FOR POINTING AND LABELING

These books are great for young children (age eighteen months to age three) who are expanding their knowledge of individual objects, animals, and items. Read these with a focus on pointing and naming what you see.

Big Red Barn by Margaret Wise Brown shows children a host of animals in the farm while describing what they do in a day in inviting rhyme.

Good Night Moon by Margaret Wise Brown is a classic for a reason. In addition to naming objects around the room, young children can also fill in the words as you read.

Everywhere Babies by Susan Meyers is a delightful book that encourages you to talk about all the things babies do in a day. You can talk about and find babies that are being carried, eating, walking, falling, and crawling.

The First 100 Words and My Big books by Roger Priddy (*First 100 Words, First 100 Animals, Farm Words, My Big Book of Animals,* and more) provide bright photo illustrations of objects, animals, and other topics that you can talk about with your child as they learn to label everything from cups to cows.

For preschoolers, books that encourage children to find specific objects are great for teaching the names of common and less common objects. Check out series like the I Spy! books, such as *I Spy Letters* by Walter Wick and *I Spy Animals* and *I Spy Numbers* by Jean Marzolo.

Also, Usborne Books' 1,001 Things to Spot series has books with an I Spy format for different topics: animals (by Ruth Broklehurst), bugs (by Emma Halbrough), on the farm (by Gillian Doherty), and more.

GREAT BOOKS FOR LETTING YOUR CHILD TAKE OVER THE STORYTELLING

Active Reading is about letting your child take the lead. These books are some of our favorites for kids to tell the story after just a few reads.

10 Minutes til Bedtime by Peggy Rathmann tells the story of a boy and his hamster friends at bedtime. The story captures how the passage of time feels at bedtime and gives lots of opportunity to point out what each hamster is doing and describe the narrative even as they count down to bedtime.

Cricket Song by Anne Hunter takes you across the world from one animal to another, showing us how we're all connected and providing lots of opportunities to talk about the animals in each picture.

First Snow by Bomi Park is the story of a young girl exploring a snowy night. There are few words but lots to discover.

Good Night, Gorilla by Peggy Rathmann is another picture book with few words but a lot of engaging illustrations that create a clear narrative for your child to use to tell the story of a bunch of zoo animals trying to sneak into a zookeeper's bedroom for the night.

Rosie's Hat by Julia Donaldson tells a simple story of what happens after Rosie's hat flies off her head. The pictures are detailed yet simple enough for young children to tell the story and find new details each time.

The books by Laura Numeroff (*If You Give a Mouse a Cookie, If You Give a Pig a Pancake*) will have your child filling in all the silly things that happen when you invite Mouse and his friends in for a treat.

GREAT BOOKS FOR ASKING QUESTIONS

These books are stories with memorable characters and clear narratives that your child can follow and that you can ask both story questions and open-ended questions about (for example guides for some of the books in this list, see appendix B).

A Sick Day for Amos McGee by Philip Stead tells the story of friendship. Ask questions about what Amos and the animals do and why.

Blueberries for Sal by Robert McClosky tells a simple story about Sal and her mother going blueberry picking, until Sal and a baby bear get mixed up on the blueberry hill.

The Corduroy books (*Corduroy, A Pocket for Corduroy*, and others) by Don Freeman tell the story of the lovable bear in green overalls and his best friend, Lisa.

Rosemary Wells is the author of many books for children, most notably for Active Reading are her Max and Ruby books that tell stories about Max and his big sister, Ruby (*Bunny Cakes, Bunny Money, Ruby's Beauty Shop, Bunny Party*, and others). There's a lot to talk about in these stories, from how we spend money to how we should treat our siblings.

Flower Garden by Eve Bunting is the story of a girl who is making her mother a birthday surprise. There's lots of opportunity to retell the story, point and name objects and colors, and connect to this story.

Knuffle Bunny by Mo Willems tells the story of Trixie who goes to the laundromat with her daddy. It's all fun and games, until Trixie leaves her beloved bunny behind.

Mike Mulligan and His Steam Shovel and other books by Virginia Lee Burton (*The Little House, Katy and the Big Snow*) are books with simple stories but with lots of detailed illustrations and multiple topics to talk about. In *The Little House*, for example, you can talk about the country versus the city or the seasons and how each looks different.

Mr. Tiger Goes Wild by Peter Brown is a fun book about a tiger who is tired of being proper. Children like seeing Mr. Tiger go from formal to his wild self, and adults can bring in the idea that it's important to be yourself.

Owl Babies by Martin Waddell tells the story of three baby owls waiting for their mom to come home. Fill in Bill's comments, talk about the story, or connect it to a time when your child had to wait for you to come home from work or an event.

Swimmy by Leo Lionni (as well as other Leo Lionni books, like *Frederick, A Color of His Own,* and *Alexander and the Wind Up Mouse*) are classic stories complemented by simple illustrations. These books are great for kids who are learning to talk about the story in addition to the pictures.

The Adventures of Beekle: The Unimaginary Friend by Dan Santat is a fun story about an imaginary friend looking for his real friend that can spark conversation about how we feel when we make a friend.

The Story of Ferdinand by Munro Leaf is the story of an introverted bull forced to fight in a bullfight in Madrid. This story is great for talking about what happens to Ferdinand and how he feels.

Three Little Pigs by Paul Galdone and other fairy tales (Paul Galdone is a wonderful illustrator, and Cynthia Rylant and Meg Park have a series of fairy tales that also have wonderful illustrations) are great for talking about and building knowledge that kids will reference as they grow.

Where the Wild Things Are by Maurice Sendak is a classic Sendak book that can be used to talk about imagination and feelings.

Wolfie the Bunny by Ame Dyckman tells the story of a wolf adopted by a bunny family. The story is funny (for adults) and engaging (for children).

GREAT BOOKS FOR BUILDING VOCABULARY

Books that are great for Active Reading (those in this appendix and others) are bound to have a few Rare Words to talk about and words that will be new to your toddler or preschooler. There are some books, though, that have more Rare Words than others.

Fancy Nancy by Jane O'Connor is a series of books about Nancy, who loves fancy words. The books have lots of Rare Words and include child-friendly definitions and connections to the stories.

I Stink by Jim McMullan and other books (*I'm Fast, I'm Dirty*) are about trucks, diggers, and cars. The books are filled with Rare Words and content-specific words (dual-op, hopper).

The Napping House by Audrey and Don Wood is an example of how synonyms can be incorporated into a book. In *The Napping House*, there are lots of different words for sleep that kids can talk about. The companion book, *The Full Moon at the Napping House*, has active words.

GREAT BOOKS FOR CONNECTING
TO EVERYDAY EXPERIENCES

Connecting to your child's world means exactly that; books that you can connect with have experiences (feelings, situations, events) that children have or will have experience with themselves. Here are some of our favorites:

With *10 Minutes til Bedtime* by Peggy Rathmann, you can compare your child's bedtime routine with what this boy and his hamsters do in the countdown to bedtime.

Hello Ocean by Pam Muñoz Ryan shows a child's day at the beach using the five senses to explore the ocean. A great book to use to connect to a child's trip to the water or to teach your child about the ocean if it isn't nearby.

Jesse Bear, What Will You Wear? by Nancy Carlstrom is a rhyming story of a little bear and what he wears throughout the day. Talk about the everyday experiences and compare them to your own day.

Anna Dewdney has written a series of books featuring Llama Llama, a young character who learns to share (*Llama Llama Time to Share*), conquer nighttime fears (*Llama Llama Red Pajama*), and go shopping without throwing temper tantrums (*Llama Llama Mad at Mama*).

The Lola books by Anna McQuinn are all about a young girl as she goes to the library (*Lola at the Library*), plants a garden (*Lola Plants a Garden*), adopts a cat (*Lola gets a Cat*), and more.

Maisy Books by Lucy Cousins are simple stories about a mouse who goes to preschool, the museum, the zoo, and other common places. Have your child retell Maisy's story, and compare what Maisy and her friends saw and did at each place with your experiences.

The Snowy Day by Ezra Jack Keats tells the story of young Peter on a snowy day in the city. This story is great for connecting to common experiences that young children experience in winter and feelings that kids may have any time. Ezra Jack Keats has written other books (*Peter's Chair, Whistle for Willie*) that are also great for Active Reading.

What Daddies Like by Judy Nevin and its partner book, *What Mommies Like*, shows the story of a young bear and his dad or mom. Children can explain what the bears are doing and connect what the bears do and how they feel with their own family experiences.

GREAT FICTION PICTURE BOOKS FOR
BUILDING BACKGROUND KNOWLEDGE

Picture books are a wonderful starting point to help children learn how the world works. Here are some favorite picture books that teach basic knowledge too:

An Orange in January by Dianna Aston tells the story of how an orange goes from tree to grocery store to snack. Use this book to talk about where food comes from and what types of workers and transportation our food sees before we eat it.

Diary of a Worm by Doreen Cronin (and other books in this series: *Diary of a Spider, Diary of a Fly*) are great introductions to the world of insects or books that you can use to connect to new information your child is learning about bugs.

Mama Built a Little Nest by Jennifer Ward shows bird nests using rhyming text. Use this book to talk about the different types of nests that birds make and how each nest helps the bird that lives there protect its young.

Leaf Jumpers by Carol Gerber is a good introductory book to use to start talking about how and why leaves turn colors and fall in autumn.

Janell Cannon's books (*Stellaluna, Verdi*, and *Pinduli*) are narratives about animals (bats, snakes, and hyenas) that show how these animals live and can be read alongside nonfiction books about these animals as well.

GREAT NONFICTION PICTURE BOOKS FOR
BUILDING BACKGROUND KNOWLEDGE

These nonfiction titles have wonderful illustrations and information about common topics that kids are interested in—the natural world, animals, weather, and more.

The Are You series by Judy Allen—including: *Are You a Ladybug? Are You a Dragonfly? Are You a Bee? Are You a Butterfly? Are You a Grasshopper? Are You an Ant? Are You a Spider?*—provide information about bugs that kids may be curious about.

Books by Dianna Hutts Aston, including *A Seed Is Sleepy*, *A Nest Is Noisy*, *A Rock Is Lively*, *An Egg Is Quiet*, and *A Butterfly Is Patient*, have beautiful illustrations and lots of Rare Words.

The Let's Read and Find Out Science Series, including *How a Seed Grows* by Helene Jordan, *From Tadpole to Frog* by Wendy Pfeffer, *Snow Is Falling* by Franklin Branley, and *Dinosaur Bones* by Aliki, explains common phenomenon with lots of pictures.

National Geographic Kids First Book series has first books of dinosaurs (by Catherine Hughes), animals (by Catherine Hughes), the ocean (by Catherine Hughes), bugs (by Karen de Seve), things that go (by Karen de Seve), weather (by Karen de Seve) and more. They provide pictures and facts about animals, habitats, and other science topics.

GREAT BOOKS FOR PICTURE WALKS

Books that have vibrant, detailed illustrations and a clear story or opportunities to talk about what's happening and use the ABCs before you read a word are great for picture walks. Here are some titles that have all those criteria:

Books by David Shannon (*Too Many Toys*, *Duck on a Bike*, *No, David!*) all capture the spirit of what it's like to be a young child with bright illustrations and simple, yet engaging, stories.

Roller Coaster by Marla Frazee is just what it sounds like—a ride on a roller coaster—which provides opportunity to talk about what's happening and how the riders are reacting, along with lots of movement words (up, down, around).

Blackout by John Rocco is a book that tells the story of what happens in one apartment building when the power goes out. Talk about what each family is doing before reading the dialogue.

Flower Garden by Eve Bunting has detailed illustrations and a simple story that make it wonderful for talking about objects (trowel, daffodil) and what the little girl is doing on each page.

Gladys Goes Out to Lunch by Derek Anderson has detailed illustrations with lots to talk about before you start reading this story about a gorilla who wants nothing more than a good meal.

Stories by Keiko Kasza (*The Wolf's Chicken Stew, My Lucky Day, The Pig's Picnic*) have simple story lines that you can talk about before you read. These are great for making predictions about what the wolf and other animals are going do to, then reading to find out what actually happens.

GREAT BOOKS FOR FILL-IN-THE-BLANK

Here are some books that lend themselves to fill-in-the-blank:

Books by Julia Donaldson (*Room on the Broom, The Gruffalo, The Gruffalo's Child*) all provide space for kids to fill-in-the-blanks of these rhyming stories.

Children can fill in monkey's tsk-tsk-tsk and the repeated phrases in *Caps for Sale* by Esphyr Slobodkina.

"I think I can, I think I can" is the repeated phrase in *The Little Engine That Could* by Watty Piper.

Have your child fill in what each animal says as the little red hen tries to bake bread in *The Little Red Hen* by Paul Galdone.

The Bear books by Karma Wilson (*Bear Snores On, Bear Feels Scared, Bear Says Thanks*) are all good ones for children to fill in the rhyming words, the animals that come visit, or how bear feels.

GREAT BOOKS FOR RHYMING AND ALLITERATION

Listening to and participating in rhymes and sounds in words helps kids learn to hear sounds in words, an important pre-reading skill. Here are some favorite books that encourage sound awareness even as they have great stories to talk about and illustrations to discuss:

Dr. Seuss books (*The Cat in the Hat, The Lorax, Green Eggs and Ham*) are classics for a reason. The stories are simple, but they are packed with rhyming word pairs and lists.

In the Small, Small Pond and *In the Tall, Tall Grass* by Denise Fleming are both books that have simple rhymes that kids can chant along with.

Jamberry by Bruce Degen is the whimsical rhythmic story of a bear and a boy delighting in berries.

Mouse Mess by Linnea Riley tells the story of a mouse that makes a mess. Find rhyming words and alliteration throughout.

The Little Blue Truck books by Alice Shertle (*Little Blue Truck*, *Little Blue Truck Leads the Way*) are both rhyming and fun stories to talk about.

Julia Donaldson books (*Room on the Broom*, *The Gruffalo*, *The Snail and the Whale*) are all written in wonderful rhyming cadence.

Rhyming Dust Bunnies by Jan Thomas is a simple, fun story about dust bunnies who can (and don't) rhyme.

Rumble in the Jungle by Giles Andreae has short poems about jungle animals.

Sheep in a Jeep by Nancy Shaw tells the story of what happens when a group of sheep drive a jeep up a hill that's steep.

Silly Sally by Audrey Wood takes kids through a rhyme about Sally and animals walking to town.

Snowmen at Night by Caralyn Buehner tells the story of what snowmen do at night, so you'll know what happened if you wake up and your snowman looks a little slumped.

Some Smug Slug by Pamela Edwards uses words that start with letter S to tell a story about a slug with a surprise ending.

GREAT BOOKS FOR LEARNING LETTERS AND ABCS

These books focus on letters. Use some of them to teach your child letters and others to expand their knowledge of letters and the words that start with each letter.

Books that introduce letters are simple, like *The Very Hungry Caterpillar ABC* by Eric Carle and *Animal Alphabet* by Alex Lluch. These books have the letter and one or two pictures (animals, foods, etc.) that start with that letter.

AlphaOops! The Day Z Went First by Althea Kontis is a great book for kids who already know their letters as the letters are out of order and the book uses humor to engage kids in the alphabet.

Chicka Chicka Boom Boom by Bill Martin is a great introduction to letters. The book has a fun rhyme, and there are lowercase and uppercase letters to talk about.

Eating the Alphabet by Lois Ehlert shows upper- and lowercase letters and fruits and vegetables to go with each.

I Stink by Jim McMullan has a list of dirty things that a garbage truck likes to eat. A is for apple cores, D is for dirty diapers, and F is for fish heads.

LMNO Peas by Keith Baker is another book to use when your child is familiar with letters. Each pea is an occupation that you can talk about to build vocabulary.

Miss Bindergarten Gets Ready for Kindergarten by Joseph Slate is a classic kindergarten story with Miss Bindergarten and her classroom of students, one for every letter of the alphabet.

Sleepy Little Alphabet by Judy Sierra shows the letters getting ready for bed. This is another book that's good for kids who are familiar with their letters and can use the pictures to find objects that start with each sound.

WORDLESS PICTURE BOOKS

Wordless picture books provide one way for kids to tell the story, and you can go as simple or deep into the illustrations as your child wants. Look for wordless picture books that connect to your child's interests or experiences.

Chalk by Bill Thomson tells the story of what can happen when chalk drawings come alive.

Fossil by Bill Thompson is about a boy who finds a fossil and what happens next.

George Shrinks by William Joyce shows the adventures of George who wakes up one day, well, shrunk.

Good Dog Carl by Alexandra Day shows what happens when a loving dog, Carl, is left in charge of the baby for the day.

Hug and *Yes* by Jez Alborough are books with simple wording and pictures that capture young children's feelings and sense of humor, even as they reinforce themes of friendship and family.

The trilogy of books by Aaron Becker—*Journey, Quest, and Return*—tell about a girl who discovers a secret world.

The Red Book by Barbara Lehman tells the story of a boy who finds a magical book that, when opened, is full of adventures.

The Treasure Bath by Dan Andresen is about what happens under the bubbles in a bathtub.

Pancakes for Breakfast by Tomie dePaola is about making pancakes for breakfast, perhaps too many!

DIVERSE BOOKS FOR ACTIVE READING

These books will provide either a mirror (a way for your child to see their experience represented in print,) or a window into someone else's experience; both are important. This is not a complete list, and new books with diverse characters are being published all the time (we're happy to say!). Check your local library and awards like the Coretta Scott King Book Awards (www.ala.org) and the Ezra Jack Keats Book Award (www.ezra-jack-keats.org), as well as organizations like We Need Diverse Books (www.diversebooks.org) for more titles and updates.

Diverse Board Books for Toddlers

10 Little Fingers and 10 Little Toes by Mem Fox shows babies from all around the world.

Baby Dance by Ann Taylor is about a daddy and daughter enjoying a spin around the living room.

Please Baby Please by Spike Lee is a board book with an African American toddler that any toddler can relate to.

The Colors of Us by Karen Katz is about a girl who notices all the different shades of brown that skin can come in during a walk around her neighborhood.

Helen Oxenbury's board books (*Tickle Tickle, Say Goodnight, Clap Hands*) always feature babies of different backgrounds and ethnicities.

There are board books about shapes and colors that celebrate different cultures: *Round Is a Mooncake, Red Is a Dragon*, and *Round Is a Tortilla* by Roseanne Thong and *Green Is a Chile Pepper* by Roseanne Greenfield.

All the World by Liz Scanlon is a poem about the importance of connectivity with beautiful illustrations.

I Like Myself by Karen Beaumont is a fun rhyme about liking every inch of yourself, down to your toes and no matter what.

Say Hello by Rachel Isadora is a celebration of the diversity of an urban neighborhood told through the experience of a little girl saying hello to all her neighbors.

Mixed Me by Taye Diggs is the story of a boy whose mom is white and dad is black.

Vera B. Williams's books (*More, More, More Said the Baby, Cherries and Cherry Pits*, and *A Chair for my Mother*) are about everyday experiences with bright, bold illustrations of diverse families.

Yoko in the picture books by Rosemary Wells (*Yoko, Yoko Finds Her Way*) tells short, sweet stories in the vein of Max and Ruby featuring Yoko, a cat with different traditions than the rest of her classmates.

Books with African American Characters

Ada Twist, Scientist by Andrea Beaty tells the story of a budding African American scientist in rhyme that rivals Dr. Seuss.

The Lola books (*Lola at the Library, Lola Gets a Cat*) by Anna McQuinn feature an African American girl in everyday situations.

Books by Ezra Jack Keats (*The Snowy Day, Peter's Chair*) feature African American characters in everyday situations.

Lisa, in *Corduroy* by Don Freeman, is an African American girl living in the city.

I Love My Hair by Natasha Tarpley is about a young girl's experience with her hair and what she likes and doesn't like about it.

Jabari Jumps by Gaia Cornwall tells the simple story of a boy jumping off the diving board for the first time. You can connect the story to swimming or when you are nervous to do something new.

Last Stop on Market Street by Matt de la Peña is a story about a young boy who goes with his grandmother on a weekly trip to a soup kitchen. This book lends itself to a lot of higher-order thinking and is best read with early elementary schoolers.

Flower Garden by Eve Bunting is the story of a young girl planting a garden box for her mother.

Rain! by Christian Robins is the delightful, simple story of a young boy on a rainy day and how a chance encounter can change our perspective.

Books with Hispanic Characters

Too Many Tamales by Gary Soto is about a young girl's experience deciding what to do after she discovers she's made a mistake. It's a great one for early elementary schoolers to connect to.

What Can You Do with a Paleta? by Carmen Tafolla is written in Spanish and English and is about an experience that every child can relate to—a visit from the ice cream cart.

Marisol McDonald Doesn't Match by Monica Brown is the story of a young girl figuring out her identity (like *Mixed Me* by Taye Diggs) and is written in both Spanish and English.

Books with Asian Characters

Dim Sum for Everyone by Grace Lin shows the experience of eating dim sum for dinner, told in bright illustrations.

Also by Grace Lin, *Kite Flying* is the story about a Chinese family's tradition of making and flying kites.

Bee Bim Bop! by Linda Sue Park is the story of a young girl making a favorite Korean family meal.

My Name Is Yoon by Helen Recorvits tells the story of how one young Korean American girl feels about writing her name in Korean and English. This book is best for children in elementary school who can relate to the experience of writing their name for their classmates to see.

Uncle Peter's Amazing Chinese Wedding by Lenore Look is the story of a young girl at her uncle's wedding and all the Chinese traditions that she experiences.

Appendix B

Active Reading Guides

$\mathcal{T}$hese guides are for classic and newer Active Reading titles that will give you some ideas of questions to ask and words to talk about. You'll notice that each guide is broken into conversations you can have the first few times you read, and conversations you can have as your child becomes familiar with the book. The ultimate goal is to have your child take over the storytelling and to use the book to engage in deeper conversations about the story. To be sure, these are not the only questions you can ask, words you can talk about, or connections you can make, but they will give you an idea of how you can engage young children in reading.

LLAMA LLAMA RED PAJAMA BY ANNA DEWDNEY

First Reading: The purpose of the first reading is to enjoy the story's rhythm and rhyming. You can also talk about what's happening to Llama Llama. When you build vocabulary in this book, have your child act out the different ways that Llama Llama communicates (he hums a tune, whimpers softly, and hollers loudly).

Ask Questions: What is Mama Llama doing in the kitchen? What does Llama Llama do when he wants his mama? What does Mama Llama do?

Build Vocabulary: hum, pout/shout

Connect to Your Child's World: What does Llama Llama do before bed? What do you do when you want your mama?

Repeated Readings: In repeated readings, in addition to helping your child tell the story themselves, you can pull out more words, practice rhyming by letting your child fill in the blanks, and talk about how Llama Llama feels.

Ask Questions: How does Llama Llama feel when his mama first goes downstairs? What does Llama think happened to Mama? What should Llama Llama do when he misses Mama? How does Mama Llama feel about little Llama? How do you know?

Build Vocabulary: whimper, moan, holler

Connect to Your Child's World: How do you feel when your mama leaves you to go to sleep? How does your mama show she loves you?

MAISY GOES TO PRESCHOOL BY LUCY COUSINS

First Reading: In a first reading, talk about what Maisy and her friends are doing at preschool and connect it to what your child does in preschool or during the day.

Ask Questions: What does Maisy do first? What do they have for snack? What are they doing that's noisy? What do they do on the playground?

Build Vocabulary: noisy

Connect to Your Child's World: What do you do at preschool? What do you have for snack at preschool? What is your favorite thing to do on the playground?

Repeated Readings: During repeated readings, ask your child to tell you what Maisy is doing and ask questions that will prompt your child to add details to their explanations.

Ask Questions: These questions will help your child add detail. Who is Maisy going to see at preschool? What art supplies do you see? What instrument is each animal playing? How does Maisy feel about preschool?

Build Vocabulary: remind

Connect to Your Child's World: What do you do at preschool that is the same as Maisy? What do you do that is different? What do you like about preschool?

NOISY NORA BY ROSEMARY WELLS

First Reading: In a first reading of *Noisy Nora*, talk about what Nora and her family are doing on each page. This gives an opportunity for your child to talk about things they may not have experienced yet (a child playing a board game, a baby getting burped).

Ask Questions: What is Nora doing? Where is Nora sitting? What did Nora do with the kite? What does the family do when they don't hear Nora anymore?

Build Vocabulary: slammed, filthy

Connect to Your Child's World: What do you do when you have to wait?
Repeated Readings: As you read *Noisy Nora* again and again, ask your child to tell you what Nora is doing and ask her how Nora feels and how her family feels. Also, have your child fill in the ends of sentences (Nora had to . . .) and the end of the story (monumental crash!). You can also ask questions that ask your child to infer, like what does your child think Mother and Kate are making (muffins).

Ask Questions: How does Nora feel? Why does she fly the kite down the stairs? How do you think her family feels when they can't find Nora?

Build Vocabulary: cellar, shrub, sifted, monumental

Connect to Your Child's World: Have you ever hidden from Mommy and Daddy? Where did you hide? What happened when you hid?

THE GRUFFALO'S CHILD BY JULIA DONALDSON

First Reading: In this rhyming story, in the first readings, talk about what the Gruffalo's child is doing and help your child anticipate which animals the Gruffalo's child will meet. (If you have read *The Gruffalo*, you may connect it to that story.) Use the pictures to show your child what words in the book mean (cave, trail, footprints, log pile).

Ask Questions: What did the Gruffalo's child do? What was happening outside? Who do you think is in the log pile house?

Build Vocabulary: terrible, trail, shadow, enormous

Connect to Your Child's World: Immediate connections could be seeing footprints in the snow or on the ground, connecting to their knowledge of animals (fox, snake, owl), and perhaps sitting on a stump.

Repeated Readings: When you are reading this book over and over, leave off the ends of sentences for your child to fill in (there are lots of rhymes that your child will have fun filling in).

Ask Questions: What does the Gruffalo's child say? What does the Gruffalo's child want to do to the mouse?

Build Vocabulary: brave, gleamed, creature, stump, beckon, boulder

Connect to Your Child's World: You can talk about what your child does when they have the feelings the Gruffalo's child does. What do they do when they are bored? What do they do when they are curious? What do they do when they feel scared?

A SEED IS SLEEPY BY DIANNA ASTON

First Reading: This is a nonfiction book that builds background knowledge about seeds as well as vocabulary related to seeds and general topics. In the first reading, explore the different types of plants and the idea of a seed, getting the big ideas (that plants grow from seeds). (This is a book that's best to read with preschoolers and kindergarteners who have the attention span and language to engage with it.)

Ask Questions: Ask questions that your child can answer by pointing or talking, such as: Which seeds are small? Which seed is big?

Build Vocabulary: Look for words that are Rare Words that you may see in other books, like *naked, adventurous, secretive.*

Connect to Your Child's World: Talk about experiences your child has had planting and growing seeds.

Repeated Readings: In repeated readings, you can talk about the big ideas and the details in this book. You can also talk more about how seeds are different from one another, and you may talk more about the diagrams that show how seeds grow.

Ask Questions: Ask about processes: What is happening to the seed? What happens first? Next? Last?

Build Vocabulary: Talk about words that are specific to seeds, like *shoot, roots,* and *coat.*

Connect to Your Child's World: You may connect to other books about seeds or plants that you've read. You may also ask your child what they want to learn about plants or seeds and extend their learning by reading books about those topics.

OWL BABIES BY MARTIN WADDELL

First Reading: The first reading is all about the sequence of the story and learning about the three owls waiting for their mother.

Ask Questions: What happened to the owl babies? Where are they?

Build Vocabulary: Talk about words that are important for understanding the story: *hunting, branch, swoop.*

Repeated Readings: In repeated readings, you can have your child fill in what Bill says on many pages ("I miss my mommy"). You can also talk about the owls' feelings as they wait for their mommy. Finally, talk about what you know about owls from this book and others that you've read.

Ask Questions: How does Bill feel? Why does he feel that way? Where do the baby owls live? What do you think the mommy owl is doing?

Build Vocabulary: Talk about feeling words, like *brave* and *fuss*.

Connect to Your Child's World: Talk about a time when your child was waiting for a parent. What did they do while they waited? How did they feel?

WHERE THE WILD THINGS ARE BY MAURICE SENDAK

First Reading: In the first reading, talk about what happens to Max and words that are important for understanding the foundation of the story—that Max is in trouble and is upset.

Ask Questions: What does Max do? Where is he going? What does Max see? What do the Wild Things do? You can also point out print knowledge, like finding the letters M, A, and X on the side of Max's boat.

Build Vocabulary: Talk about the words at the start of the book, like *mischief*, and words that are important for understanding characters, like *wild*.

Connect to Your Child's World: Talk about a time that your child acted naughty and what happened to them.

Repeated Readings: As you read the book over and over, talk about how Max feels and how the Wild Things feel and have your child fill in parts of the book. For example, when the Wild Things gnash their terrible teeth and show their terrible claws. And when Max says, "Stop!"

Ask Questions: How does Max feel when he's in time-out? How does he feel after he meets the Wild Things? How does Max feel at the end of the story?

Build Vocabulary: Talk about words in the middle of the story, like *gnashed, terrible, claws*.

Connect to Your Child's World: Talk about a time when your child started out feeling one way and then ended feeling another. What did he do to change how he felt? What helped him?

ROSIE'S HAT BY JULIA DONALDSON

First Reading: Talk about what's happening in the pictures. What happens to Rosie and to her hat? You may have your child point to the hat and talk about what it's doing in each picture.

Ask Questions: What is Rosie doing? Where did the hat go? What tickled the dog's nose? What did the dog do? Who is in the tree?

Build Vocabulary: Talk about nouns that your child may not know, like *cliff, feather, beak*. Use the pictures to help explain each word.

Connect to Your Child's World: Ask questions that connect your child's experiences to the story, like: What does Rosie become when she grows up? Do you know any fire fighters? Have you ever seen fire fighters? What do fire fighters do?

Repeated Readings: Encourage your child to tell the story or fill in the repeated words on each page. You can also ask questions about why the animals and people do what they do in the story.

Ask Questions: What happened? What's going to happen next? What will the boys do with the hat? Why did the mouse run under the hat?

Build Vocabulary: Talk about action words that your child does not know, like *dash, flutters, tossed*.

Connect to Your Child's World: You can talk about a time when you lost something. Where did it go? Encourage your child to imagine what happened to the object they lost. Who might have it now? Where might your child find it again?

BUNNY MONEY BY ROSEMARY WELLS

First Reading: In the first reading, talk about what happens to Max and Ruby and name any objects that your child may not be familiar with yet.

Ask Questions: What is Max doing? What is Ruby doing? What does Ruby want? What does Max want? What does Max buy? What does Ruby buy?

Build Vocabulary: Talk about words that are important for understanding the story, like *quarter, wallet, vampire teeth*, and *wrapping paper*.

Connect to Your Child's World: You can introduce the idea of money through this book, talk about the money that Ruby has in her wallet, and count how many bills are left after each purchase.

Repeated Readings: When you read this story again, encourage your child to talk about how Max and Ruby are spending the money—your child may like to count the dollars in Ruby's wallet each time you read. Also, talk about cause and effect and the sequence of the events in the story.

Ask Questions: What does Max spend the money on? Is this a good idea? Why does Ruby take Max to the laundromat?

Build Vocabulary: Talk about descriptive words like *oozing*. Also, talk about phrases like "down the drain" to start exposing your child to the idea of idioms and how to understand common phrases. You can also talk about money phrases, like "half price."

Connect to Your Child's World: This book offers the opportunity to talk about when you and your child have gone shopping. Did you find things on sale? Did you have a list of things to buy? What presents have you bought for friends and family? How did they like the present you bought? How is that similar to how Grandma felt when she got the gifts from Max and Ruby?

RUMBLE IN THE JUNGLE BY GILES ANDREAE

First Reading: *Rumble in the Jungle* is not a story but a collection of poems about jungle animals. In the first reading, read the book to experience the rhymes and talk about each animal. You can find out what your child already knows about each animal.

Ask Questions: Ask questions about each animal. What color is the gorilla? Is the giraffe tall or short? Which animals are tall? Which animals are short? What does the hippo like to do?

Build Vocabulary: Talk about words related to each animal and what each poem teaches about the animal. For example, you may define fleas and how chimpanzees eat fleas. You may also talk about what a jungle is and what types of animals live in a jungle.

Connect to Your Child's World: If you have visited a zoo, you can talk about animals you've seen and what you know about those animals already: Remember when we went to the zoo and saw a zebra; what was the zebra doing?

Repeated Readings: In repeated readings, have your child find the rhyming words in each poem (which word rhymes with *night?*). They can also create lists of rhyming words using the poems as a start: What rhymes with *fear* and *near?*

Ask Questions: Ask questions about why the author created each rhyme. For example, why do the other animals "shudder and shiver" when the lion roars?

Build Vocabulary: Talk about Rare Words (*rumble*), adjectives (*handsome*), and verbs (*shudders* and *shivers*).

Connect to Your Child's World: Connect the rhymes to information that your child knows about animals, like that some animals are nocturnal and only come out at night. Which nocturnal animals are in this book? What do they do?

BEEKLE: THE UNIMAGINARY FRIEND BY DAN SANTAT

First Reading: Beekle is the story of an imaginary friend who is in search of a real friend. In the first reading, talk about the important characters, Beekle and Alice, and the locations in the book, the island, the city, the park.

Ask Questions: Where is Beekle? What is Beekle doing? Who does he see? Who does he meet?

Build Vocabulary: In the first readings, you may want to talk about real versus imaginary. There are also Rare Words, like *brave* and *familiar.*

Connect to Your Child's World: Depending on your child's age, you can talk about how they met a friend or who their friends are.

Repeated Readings: In repeated readings of *Beekle*, you can delve deeper into the story, the illustrations, and talking about Beekle's experiences as he travels from the imagined to the real world.

Ask Questions: The illustrations provide a lot of details. You may talk about how the illustrations of the city are dark and brown, until Beekle gets to the park and then they are bright. You can also talk about how Beekle or Alice is feeling as he moves through the story: And now that you know Alice is waiting for him, how might Alice feel?

Build Vocabulary: If your child is ready for it, you can talk about the words *unimaginable* (or impossible) and *unimaginary* and how these words are used in the book. For example, Beekle does the unimaginable, and Beekle is an unimaginary (or real) friend.

Connect to Your Child's World: Talk about the feelings in the story and when your child has felt similarly. Did your child ever meet someone who "felt just right"? Who was that person? Or has your child ever felt brave? What did they do when they felt brave?

LITTLE BLUE TRUCK LEADS THE WAY BY ALICE SHERTLE

First Reading: In the first reading, talk about what Little Blue sees in the city and what he does.

Ask Questions: Ask questions that draw your child's attention to the pictures. Where is the city? What other cars do you see?

Build Vocabulary: Talk about words that describe the city, like *high, fast, avenue, horn, blast, siren.*

Connect to Your Child's World: If you live in or have visited a big city, you can talk about what you saw in the city. Did you see tall buildings and a traffic jam? If you have not been to the city, talk about the things you see in your town that are similar. Do you see buses? Have you ever seen a limo in your town? As you walk and drive around your town, what do you see that you saw in *Little Blue*? Is there a garbage truck? A double decker bus?

Repeated Readings: As you read this book again and again, encourage your child to talk about each picture, notice more details (like the skunks crossing the road on the first page), and talk about the lesson in the story.

Ask Questions: Ask questions that encourage your child to talk about how Little Blue feels and what he teaches the other trucks. What did the grocery truck do? How is he acting? What does Little Blue think of this? What does Little Blue want everyone to do? Why is that a good idea?

Build Vocabulary: Have your child fill in the blanks with rhyming words and other words, like the noises the cars make. You may also pull out some Rare Words, like *hollering, tangle, wrangle*.

Connect to Your Child's World: This is a great book to connect to other activities, like lining up cars in a traffic jam or orderly line during play time. Or draw a map of a city with different types of buildings, then use toy cars to navigate through the city.

10 MINUTES TIL BEDTIME BY PEGGY RATHMANN

First Reading: *10 Minutes til Bedtime* is an (almost) wordless picture book about bedtime. The first time through, talk about what's happening on each page, and follow your child's lead about what they want to talk about.

Ask Questions: What is the boy doing? What is the dad doing? What are the hamsters doing?

Build Vocabulary: The opportunity to build vocabulary in this book is in the pictures. Point out things in the pictures that your child may not be able to name yet, like the types of boats and bath toys that the hamsters are playing with in the tub or the different types of vehicles that they arrive in (a camper, double decker bus, etc.).

Connect to Your Child's World: Talk about what your child does before bed that is similar to the boy in this story. Do you get snacks, take a bath, brush teeth in the same order or a different order?

Repeated Readings: As you continue to read *10 Minutes til Bedtime*, talk about the details. Each hamster has a personality, and you can choose one hamster to focus on. Or you may find that your child has a way they like to "read" the story to you. Let them!

Ask Questions: What is each hamster doing? What is happening on this page? How does the little boy feel?

Connect to Your Child's World: Talk about how it feels to go to bed. Does it feel like you have a lot of time until it's almost bedtime? Do you ever feel like the little boy when you just want everyone to leave so you can go to bed? You can also use this story to encourage your child to tell their own stories about what they would do if they had a hamster (or favorite animal) join them during bedtime.

Appendix C

Building a Coordinated System of Active Reading in Your Community

*I*n early 2015, local leaders in Charlotte, North Carolina, launched a new children's initiative called Read Charlotte with a bold mission: to double third-grade reading proficiency from 39 percent in 2015 to 80 percent in 2025.[1] Helping parents to develop children's early language and literacy skills is one of the initiative's key pillars for action. Read Charlotte is one of more than three hundred community initiatives around the country in the Campaign for Grade Level Reading focused on improving early literacy from birth through third grade. We've had the privilege of working together to help to launch this important community initiative.

In Read Charlotte's early days, we spent more than one thousand hours wading through two dozen databases and hundreds of research papers to find evidence-based practices and programs proven to move the needle for children for early language and literacy outcomes. The research that underpins Active Reading is plentiful and dates to the 1980s.

There are many rigorous studies that demonstrate that the strategies outlined in this book help build young children's language, vocabulary, and comprehension skills. The main problem was that no one had successfully translated this research into information that could be easily understood and used by parents, librarians, and educators. This book is intended to help fill this gap.

Although the advice in this book focuses primarily on how to do Active Reading one-on-one or with small groups of children, we believe it is possible to develop a coordinated system of Active Reading in your community to benefit even more children. In this section, we offer suggestions for community organizations and leaders about how to broadly promote and support

Active Reading in a way that builds upon existing programs and systems in your community.

PROMOTE ACTIVE READING AS A PRACTICE,
NOT A PROGRAM

Active Reading is best understood as a *practice* that can be embedded into the fabric of your community. It's not a new program but rather a new way of using children's picture books you likely already have in your community and enhancing the time families, teachers, and volunteers already spend reading with children.

You don't need to—and you shouldn't have to—start a new organization in your community to promote Active Reading. Organizations in your community don't have to drop what they're doing to start to infuse these strategies into their existing programs. *Any touchpoint with young children and families* offers an opportunity to begin to promote Active Reading as a way to use picture books more effectively to build children's language and early literacy skills.

USE ACTIVE READING TO STRENGTHEN CONNECTIONS
WITH CHILDREN'S HOMES

Including families in the development of their children's language and literacy skills is an incredibly powerful way to increase the impact of local programs in your community. But this admittedly is easier said than done, and community groups and schools struggle to engage and involve families in many initiatives. This is particularly true for groups seeking to reach minority, low-income, and non-native-English-speaking families. We think Active Reading can help bridge this divide.

Active Reading taps into families' desire to help their children succeed. It provides families with actionable steps they can take to help their children be successful in school. But getting this information out in your community may require a different way of thinking about how to connect with some of the families you want to serve. We suggest that rather than *engaging* or *educating* families, you approach this as *empowering* them with a set of proven strategies to develop their children's early literacy skills. This means making sure the approaches you take to promote Active Reading in your community actually work for the families you want to support. And this probably will require talking with and listening to families to figure out the most effective ways to do this in your community.

Yes, this likely will take additional work. But at the end of the rainbow is a common framework and shared vocabulary for parents, caregivers, preschool teachers, and elementary teachers across your community to work together to support children's reading development. For children, Active Reading becomes even more powerful when the literacy routines they experience at home are mirrored in the classroom and community programs. This is more than worth the time and effort required to figure this out for your community.

LEVERAGE NATIONAL PROGRAMS THAT OPERATE IN YOUR COMMUNITY

There are a number of national organizations that focus on families and/or literacy that may be operating in your community: Dolly Parton Imagination Library, Reach Out and Read, Raising a Reader, First Book, Parents as Teachers, HIPPY, Motheread/Fatheread, and the Campaign for Grade Level Reading to name a few.

Look for opportunities to leverage your local community's investment in these programs and the capacity that they bring. If these groups provide books to children or families, you can help families use Active Reading strategies to get more out of the time they spend reading these books with their children. For example, you might provide opportunities to share Active Reading strategies with families that participate in the Raising a Reader program that sends red-colored bags of books home weekly. You can also look for opportunities to integrate Active Reading within programs like Raising a Reader and Head Start that have a family engagement component. Active Reading can also inform programs in which families are encouraged to read with their kids. For example, Active Reading can be included in local training of staff that make home visits or medical providers participating in the Reach Out and Read program.

EMBED ACTIVE READING PRACTICES WITHIN LOCAL PROGRAMS THAT ALREADY HAVE A FOCUS ON READING

One of the fastest ways to promote Active Reading in your community is through local programs that are already focused on literacy. In our experience, it's sometimes easier for locally grown programs to incorporate new ideas like Active Reading than local branches of national programs, which may need to secure permission from their national offices. (In fairness, their focus is probably on fidelity to the national model, which is especially important for evidence-based interventions.)

For example, many communities have "reading buddy" programs that pair volunteers who read with young children. In our experience, these types of local programs often provide limited training for volunteers. Training the volunteers in Active Reading provides an opportunity to increase the impact of these programs, helping volunteers feel more confident and better prepared and offering greater benefits for the time children spend in the program. If this is something that you're going to explore, don't forget to investigate whether these programs need to purchase different children's picture books better aligned to support Active Reading strategies. (See appendix A for book ideas.)

EMBED ACTIVE READING WITHIN LOCAL PROGRAMS NOT FOCUSED ON READING

There are likely groups in your community that do not currently focus on reading but could incorporate Active Reading into some of their program offerings. Groups like the YMCA, Boys and Girls Clubs, and YWCA often have times in their children's programming that could offer opportunities for Active Reading–trained staff and volunteers to read with children. Other groups like Big Brothers Big Sisters pair volunteer mentors with children.

There is a similar opportunity to train these adult volunteers in Active Reading strategies that support the mission of these mentoring organizations. Active Reading offers an opportunity to use children's picture books to open up conversations, explore ideas, and make connections with children. And don't overlook places where parents and caregivers routinely bring children. Active Reading–trained volunteers can read with children in waiting rooms of doctor offices or other places where families routinely and predictably wait in line for services (e.g., DMVs, WIC offices, courthouses, etc.).

EMBED ACTIVE READING IN SUMMER AND OUT-OF-SCHOOL PROGRAMS

After-school programs often have the challenge of creating engaging activities for children that don't feel like an extension of the school day but yet still provide bona fide academic support and enrichment. By actively engaging children in conversation, getting them talking about how the books relate to their experiences, Active Reading helps make reading time in after-school programs fun and engaging. This also offers needed "energy" to children at the end of a long day.

Summer programs are an especially great opportunity for Active Reading. Staff and volunteers can be trained to use Active Reading strategies. We've seen seniors in a retirement home and teenage summer camp counselors use Active Reading with children over the summer both in one-on-one and group settings.

We've seen traditional summer camps that offer sports and crafts successfully infuse an hour of literacy in part by using Active Reading strategies. Out-of-school and summer organizations with a STEM or STEAM focus can especially benefit from using Active Reading to add an effective literacy component to their programs. Active Reading can support project-based learning, using hands-on activities to build and reinforce concepts, facts, and vocabulary that children encounter in carefully selected books.

GET YOUR LOCAL LIBRARY INVOLVED

The library has a big role to play to promote Active Reading in your community. In many communities, the library is a trusted resource not only for books but advice about reading for parents and caregivers. Families of young children often are accustomed to going to the local library for story time or storytelling events. But as you know by now, Active Reading is not the best way to lead a story time, nor is it the same as storytelling.

In Charlotte, North Carolina, the Charlotte Mecklenburg Library has trained more than one hundred librarians in Active Reading strategies and offers workshops across its twenty library branches for families in how to do Active Reading with their children. Across the county, children's librarians also help families find books that are good for Active Reading at home.

LEVERAGE LOCAL FINANCIAL RESOURCES
FOR FAMILY ENGAGEMENT

Some organizations have funds that they are required to use to do outreach to the families they serve. For example, elementary schools that receive federal Title I funds are required to use some of these dollars to engage families. Federally funded Head Start child-care centers also have to convene families regularly. Using these opportunities to empower families with Active Reading strategies supports the goals and missions of these organizations.

Inquire if any of the local organizations in your community that support families of young children have budget line items for family engagement and are open to or looking for ideas on how to engage families. This can be an important financial resource to leverage to support training for families in Active Reading. For example, these funds sometimes can be used to pay for books, handouts, meals, or other costs needed to offer Active Reading training for families they serve. The best opportunities are where Active Reading helps fulfill a family engagement requirement that local organizations have to meet. Partnering with these groups can create a win–win for your community.

The goal of building a coordinated system of Active Reading should be to ensure that children in your community experience Active Reading at home, in child-care programs, in elementary school, and in out-of-school programs. It can support local efforts to increase early childhood development and promote school readiness. A community-wide approach to promote Active Reading should leverage existing efforts that offer home visits to new families or provide high-quality preschool.

In Charlotte, we're seeing Active Reading embraced by the public library, school district, child-care programs, and nonprofit agencies. Volunteers are being trained in Active Reading strategies as part of school-based and community-based reading programs. Active Reading is being incorporated into summer programs and family engagement strategies in our community. Active Reading offers a practical way to increase families' awareness of early literacy and provides specific ways that they can support their children at home. It provides an entry point to volunteers to read with children in ways that can help them down the pathway to reading proficiency. And for the children themselves, it can help build an early love of books and reading that can last a lifetime. Now what could be better than that?

Glossary

ABCs of Active Reading: An evidence-based way of reading with children to build language, vocabulary, and comprehension. The ABCs include: Ask questions, Build vocabulary, and Connect a book with a child's world.

Active Reading: An evidence-based way to read with a child rather than to them. The focus is on creating a conversation about the book, using the pictures and story to build a child's vocabulary and engage them in questions that get them talking about the story and how it relates to their life. (Also known as "dialogic reading," "interactive shared reading," or "shared reading.")

Alphabet Knowledge: A child's knowledge that letters represent spoken sounds and of letter names and letter sounds. (Also known as "alphabetic principle.")

Background Knowledge: All the information a child has and uses to understand conversations, stories, text, and other media. The more a child knows, the easier it is to learn new things.

Blending: The ability to put sounds together to make words. This is a key phonemic awareness skill that children use when they begin to read on their own.

Common Words (aka Tier 1 words): Words that are used in everyday language (*yummy*, *blue*, *hat*) and that are the most basic or commonly used form of any word. Common Words typically do not have multiple meanings.

Compare and Contrast Questions: Questions that ask children to think about how things are similar and different.

Comprehension: Reading comprehension is the ability to understand what is read, including skills like making inferences. Comprehension requires being able to understand the words you read, reading "between the lines" to make inferences, and reading "beyond the lines" to draw connections

155

to bigger ideas and concepts. Children understand what they read when they combine their background knowledge, or what they know about the world, with information from the text.

Consequence Questions: Questions that ask "what if" help readers think about different ways the same character or story information could be different.

Evaluation Questions: Questions that ask children to form an opinion about whether something that happened in a story was right or wrong.

Evidence-Based: A practice or program that has been tested to show demonstrated improvements for a group of children on a specific outcome compared to a similar group of children who received an alternative practice or program.

Expressive Language: The ability to put thoughts into words and sentences in a way that makes sense and is grammatically accurate.

Fill-in-the-Blank: A type of completion prompt in which adults leave off parts of the text for children to fill in. For example, an adult might let a child fill in the sounds that an animal makes or complete the dialogue in a familiar book. This technique increases both expressive and receptive language skills.

Flat Characters: Characters whose responses, attitudes, and actions do not change regardless of the situation.

Fluency: The speed, accuracy (number of words read correctly), and expression that a child has when reading. Fluent reading, when text is read easily and with expression, is enjoyable to listen to, like how a television anchor sounds when she reads the news or how an audiobook sounds. Fluency is strongly related to comprehension, since when children struggle to read one word at a time, they are unable to gain a broader understanding of the sentences and paragraphs they are reading.

Inference Questions: Questions that ask children to combine prior knowledge with information from the book to build meaning (or infer ideas, actions, or insights) from the text (see Comprehension).

Joint Attention: When an adult and child are focusing on the same thing (picture, character, event, etc.) in a book for a period of time. The simple act of following what the child is interested in and talking about that increases the number of words a child learns.

Kid-Friendly Definition: A way to define a word using vocabulary and ideas that a child has already mastered so that the child understands the new word.

Knowledge Words (aka Tier 3 words): Low-frequency, content-specific words that are used in specific school subjects, hobbies, occupations, geographic regions, technology, weather, etc. (e.g., science words like *atom*, *microscope*, and *prehistoric*).

Literacy Routines: Intentional, structured ways frequently used to build language and literacy skills in children. Active Reading is a type of literacy routine, a specific set of practices used when reading a book with a child. Children come to know and expect these practices when reading a book.

Onset: The first sound in a word, which consists of the initial consonant or consonant blend. For example, in the word *car*, the sound /c/ is the onset. In the word *clean*, the sound /cl/ is the onset.

Open-Ended Question: Questions that require more than a "yes" or "no" response and have answers that cannot be found just in the story or text. Open-ended questions ask a child to connect with the text based upon their prior knowledge and experiences. Open-ended questions require more thinking than story questions.

Oral Language: A large set of skills that encompasses listening comprehension, understanding and producing complex language, vocabulary and word knowledge, grammatical knowledge, phonological skills, and more.

Phonemic Awareness: The ability to hear, identify, and manipulate individual sounds in words. Phonemes are the smallest segments of sounds. For example, the word *cat* has three phonemes: /c/ /a/ /t/. A child with strong phonemic awareness can identify other words that start with the /c/ sound (like *car* or *candle*) or other words that end with the sounds /a/ /t/ (like *mat* or *rat*).

Phonics: The understanding that letters and combinations of letters represent sounds that come together to make words. Phonics is the understanding of how written letters translate into spoken language.

Picture Walk: A way of introducing a child to stories through talking about the pictures and illustrations in a book.

Prediction Questions: Questions that ask readers to anticipate what will come next in a story using their knowledge of the story to make that decision.

Print Concepts: A child's understanding of how to hold a book, how to turn the pages, and how to start looking at the pages (from left to right)

Print Knowledge: A child's understanding of how words written on the page hold meaning and how to read them (from left to right and that we loop down and continue at the end of a line or sentence).

Problem-Solving Questions: Questions that encourage readers to think about alternative ways a character in a book could solve a problem. For example, "What else could the character have done? What would have happened if they solved the problem that way?"

Rare Words (aka Tier 2 words): Words that are used more often in written language and are sometimes synonyms to Common Words but are used less frequently in spoken language (e.g., *delicious*, *navy*, *beret*). Rare Words occur often in mature language situations such as adult conversations and literature and therefore strongly influence speaking and reading. Rare Words often have multiple meanings.

Receptive Language: The ability to understand words, sentences, and meaning of what others say or what is read.

Right Here Question: A vocabulary-building question that refers a child to a specific picture or word in a story to learn or use a new or familiar word.

Rime: A rime is the part of a syllable that consists of its vowel and any consonant sounds that come after it. For example, in the word *den*, the sound /en/ makes up the rime.

Round Characters: Characters that are changing and dynamic like real people. They may act one way in one situation and another way in a different situation.

Segmenting: The ability to break words down into individual sounds. For example, the word *run* is made up of three individual phonemes or sounds: /r/, /u/, and /n/.

Stop and Think Question: A vocabulary-building question that asks a child to use information (from other stories, from their experience, or through more abstract thinking) that does not come right from the book to answer a question about the meaning or use of a word.

Story Question: A closed question about the parts of the story (characters, settings, events) with an answer from the story, words, or pictures in the book. Story questions can be answered using information from the text or story. No matter how many times you read the book the answer is always the same.

Talk More: A sequence of questions and prompts by adults during Active Reading that shows children how to use language correctly, gives them more language and vocabulary about the topic they are talking about, and encourages them to expand their thinking.

Vocabulary: A child's knowledge of words, including the number of words they know and how well they understand each word. A child may have a basic understanding of a word (that an engine is something that makes a vehicle go) or a deep understanding (that there are many types of engines and that an engine can refer to what makes something happen).

Notes

INTRODUCTION

1. Hernandez, D. J. (April 2011). *Double jeopardy: How third-grade reading skills and poverty influence high school graduation.* Baltimore: Annie E. Casey Foundation. Retrieved September 8, 2016, from: www.aecf.org/resources/double-jeopardy/.

2. Hernandez, 2011.

3. Lonigan, C. J., & Whitehurst, G. J. (1998). Relative efficacy of parent and teacher involvement in a shared-reading intervention for preschool children from low-income backgrounds. *Early Childhood Research Quarterly, 13,* 263–290.

4. Mol, S. E., Bus, A. G., & de Jong, M. T. (2009). Interactive book reading in early education: A tool to stimulate print knowledge as well as oral language. *Review of Educational Research, 79,* 979–1007.

5. What Works Clearinghouse. (2010). *What Works Clearinghouse intervention report: Early childhood education intervention for children with disabilities: Dialogic reading.* Washington, DC: Institute for Education Sciences. Retrieved from: ies.ed.gov/ncee/wwc/interventionreport/136.

CHAPTER 1

1. Lonigan & Whitehurst, 1998.

2. Names have been changed.

3. Lonigan & Whitehurst, 1998.

4. Whitehurst, G. J., Arnold D. S., Epstein, J. N., Angell, A. L., Smith, M., & Fischel, J. E. (1994). A picture book reading intervention in day care and home for children from low-income families. *Developmental Psychology, 30,* 679–689; Whitehurst, G. J., Falco, F. L., Lonigan, C. J., & Fischel, J. E. (1988). Accelerating language development through picture book reading. *Developmental Psychology, 24,* 552–559.

5. National Early Literacy Panel. (2008). *Developing early literacy: Report of the Early Literacy Panel*. Retrieved from: https://lincs.ed.gov/publications/pdf/NELPReport09 .pdf.

6. Fung, P., Chow, B. W., & McBride-Chang, C. (2005). The impact of a dialogic reading program on deaf and hard-of-hearing kindergarten and early primary school-aged students in Hong Kong. *The Journal of Deaf Studies and Deaf Education, 10,* 82–95; Valdez-Menchaca, M. C., & Whitehurst, G. J. (1992). Accelerating language development through picture book reading: A systematic extension to Mexican day care. *Developmental Psychology, 28,* 1106–1114; Whitehurst et al., 1988; Whitehurst et al., 1994.

7. Wasik, B. A., & Bond, M. A. (2001). Beyond the pages of a book: Interactive book reading and language development in preschool classrooms. *Journal of Educational Psychology, 93,* 243–250; Wasik, B. A., Bond, M. A., & Hindman, A. (2006). The effects of a language and literacy intervention in Head Start children and teachers. *Journal of Educational Psychology, 98,* 63–74.

8. Valdez-Menchaca & Whitehurst, 1992; Zevenbergen, A. A., Worth, S., Pretto, D., & Travers, K. (2016). Parents' experiences in a home-based dialogic reading programme. *Early Child Development and Care,* 1–13.

9. Wasik & Bond, 2001; Wasik et al., 2006.

10. Whitehurst et al., 1988.

11. Arnold, D. H., Lonigan, C., Whitehurst, G. J., & Epstein, J. N. (1994). Accelerating language development through picture book reading: Replication and extension to a videotape training format. *Journal of Educational Psychology, 86,* 235–243; Whitehurst et al., 1994.

12. Arnold, D. H., Whitehurst, G. J., Epstein, J. N, Angell, A. L., Smith, M., & Fischel, J. E. (1994). A picture book reading intervention in day care and home for children from low-income families. *Developmental Psychology, 30,* 679–689.

13. Dickinson, D. K., & Porche, M. V. (2011). Relation between language experiences in preschool classrooms and children's kindergarten and fourth-grade language and reading abilities. *Child Development, 82,* 870–886.

14. Lefebvre, P., Trudeau, N., & Sutton, A. (2011). Enhancing vocabulary, print awareness, and phonological awareness through shared storybook reading with low-income preschoolers. *Journal of Early Childhood Literacy, 11,* 453–479.

15. Burgess, S. (1997). The role of shared reading in the development of phonological awareness: A longitudinal study of middle and upper class children. *Early Child Development and Care, 127/128,* 191–199; Lefebvre et al., 2011.

16. Senechal, M., Thomas, E., & Moner, J. A. (1995). Individual differences in 4-year-old children's acquisition of vocabulary during storybook reading. *Journal of Educational Psychology, 87,* 218-229; Tomasello, M., & Farrar, M. J. (1986). Joint attention and early language. *Child Development, 57,* 1454–1463.

17. Hoff-Ginsburg, E. (1991). Mother-child conversation in different social classes and communicative settings. *Child Development, 62,* 782–796; Weizman, Z, & Snow, C. (2001). Lexical input as related to children's vocabulary acquisition: Effects of sophisticated exposure and support for meaning. *Developmental Psychology, 37,* 265–279.

18. Whitehurst et al., 1988.

19. Ard, L. M. & Beverly, B. L. (2004). Preschool word learning during joint book reading: Effect of adult questions and comments. *Communication Disorders Quarterly, 26,* 17–28; Walsh, B. A., & Blewitt, P. (2006). The effect of questioning style during storybook reading on novel vocabulary acquisition of preschoolers. *Early Childhood Education Journal, 33,* 273–278.

20. Wasik et al., 2006.

21. van Kleeck, A., Vander Woude, J., & Hammett, L. (2006). Fostering literal and inferential language skills in Head Start preschoolers with language impairment using scripted book sharing discussions. *American Journal of Speech-Language Pathology, 15,* 1–11.

22. Cain, K., Oakhill, J., & Bryant, P. (2004). Children's reading comprehension ability: Concurrent prediction by working memory, verbal ability, and component skills. *Journal of Educational Psychology, 96,* 31–42; Nation, K., & Snowling, M. J. (2004). Beyond phonological skills: Broader language skills contribute to the development of reading. *Journal of Research in Reading, 27,* 342–356.

23. Cain et al., 2004; Nation & Snowling, 2004.

24. Ravid, D., & Tolchinsky, L. (2002). Developing linguistic literacy: A comprehensive model. *Journal of Child Language, 29,* 417–447.

25. Wasik et al., 2006.

26. Kaefer, T., Neuman, S. B., & Pinkham, A. M. (2015). Pre-existing background knowledge influences socioeconomic differences in preschoolers' word learning and comprehension. *Reading Psychology, 36,* 203–231.

27. Fenson et al. (1994). Variability in early communicative development. *Monographs of the Society for Research in Child Development, 59,* i–85.

28. Godfield, B. A., & Reznick, J. S. (1990). Early lexical acquisition: Rate, content, and the vocabulary spurt. *Journal of Child Language, 17,* 177–183.

29. University of Iowa. (2007, August 3). Why do children experience a vocabulary explosion at 18 months of age? *Science Daily.* Retrieved from: www.sciencedaily.com /releases/2007/08/070802182054.htm.

30. Wells, G. (1985). *Language development in the preschool years.* New York: Cambridge University Press.

31. Leseman, P., & de Jong, P. G. (1998). Home literacy: Opportunity, instruction, cooperation, and social-emotional quality predicting early reading achievement. *Reading Research Quarterly, 33,* 294–318.

CHAPTER 2

1. Duncan, G. J., Claessens, A., Huston, A. C., Pagani, L. S., Engel, M., Sexton, H., et al. (2007). School readiness and later achievement. *Developmental Psychology, 43,* 1428–1446; Roberts, T. A. (2011). Preschool foundations for reading and writing success. In R. E. O'Connor & P. F. Vadasy (Eds.), *Handbook of reading interventions.* New York: Guilford Press.

2. Hernandez, 2011.

3. Hernandez, 2011.

4. Hernandez, 2011.

5. National Center for Educational Statistics. (2015). *National assessment of educational progress.* U.S. Department of Education. Retrieved from: http://nces.ed.gov/nationsreportcard.

6. National Center for Educational Statistics, 2015.

7. National Reading Panel. (2000). *Report of the National Reading Panel: Teaching children to read: An evidence-based assessment of the scientific research literature on reading and its implications for reading instruction: reports of the subgroups.* Washington, DC: National Institute of Child Health and Human Development, National Institutes of Health.

8. Adams, M. (1990). *Beginning to read: Thinking and learning about print.* Cambridge, MA: MIT Press; Stanovich, K. E. (1986). Matthew effects in reading: Some consequences of individual differences in the acquisition of literacy. *Reading Research Quarterly, 21,* 360–406.

9. Cain, K., Oakhill, J., & Lemmon, K. (2004). Individual differences in the inference of word meaning from context: The influence of reading comprehension, vocabulary knowledge, and memory capacity. *Journal of Educational Psychology, 96,* 571–681.

10. Lonigan, C. J., Burgess, S. R., & Anthony, J. L. (2000). Development of emergent and early reading skills in preschool children: Evidence from a latent-variable longitudinal study. *Developmental Psychology, 36,* 596–613.

11. Ezell, H., & Justice, L. M. (2005). *Shared storybook reading: Building young children's language and emergent literacy skills.* Baltimore, MD: Brookes Publishing.

12. Ezell & Justice, 2005.

13. Girolametto, L., & Weitzman, E. (2002). Responsiveness of childcare providers in interactions with toddlers and preschoolers. *Language, Speech, and Hearing Services in Schools, 33,* 268–281.

14. McGinty, A. S., & Justice, L. M. (2009). Predictors of print knowledge in children with specific language impairment: Experiential and developmental factors. *Journal of Speech, Language, and Hearing Research, 52,* 81–97.

15. Dickinson & Porche, 2011; Tomasello, M., & Farrar, M. J. (1986). Joint attention and early language. *Child Development, 57,* 1454–1463.

16. Girolametto & Weitzman, 2002.

17. Roberts, J., Jurgens, J., & Burchinal, M. (2005). The role of home literacy practices in preschool children's language and emergent literacy skills. *Journal of Speech, Language, and Hearing Research, 48,* 345–359; Bus, A., & van Ijzendoorn, M. (1988). Mother-child interactions, attachment, and emerging literacy: A cross-sectional study. *Child Development, 59,* 1262–1272.

18. Senechal, M., & LeFevre, J. (2002). Parental involvement in the development of children's reading skill: A five-year longitudinal study. *Child Development, 73,* 445-460.

19. Storch, S. A., & Whitehurst, G. J. (2002). Oral language and code-related precursors to reading: Evidence from a longitudinal structural model. *Developmental Psychology, 38,* 934–947.

20. Cain, K. (1996). Story knowledge and comprehension skill. In C. Cornoldi & J. V. Oakhill (Eds.), *Reading comprehension difficulties: Processes and intervention* (pp. 167–192). Mahwah, NJ: Erlbaum.

21. Cain, 1996.

22. Ezell & Justice, 2005; Justice, L. M., McGinty, A. S., Piasta, S. B, Kaderavek, J. N., & Fan, X. (2010). Print focused read-alouds in preschool classrooms: Intervention effectiveness and moderators of child outcomes. *Language, Speech, and Hearing Services in Schools, 41,* 504–521.

23. Snow, C. E., Burns, M. S. & Griffin, P. (Eds.). (1998). *Preventing reading difficulties in young children.* Washington, DC: National Academy Press.

24. Mol, S. E., Bus, A. G., & de Jong, M. T. (2009). Interactive book reading in early education: A tool to stimulate print knowledge as well as oral language. *Review of Educational Research, 79,* 979–1007.

25. Phillips, G., & McNaughton, S. (1990). The practice of storybook reading to preschool children in mainstream New Zealand families. *Reading Research Quarterly, 25,* 196–212.

CHAPTER 3

1. Isbell, R. T. (2002). Telling and retelling stories: Language and literacy. *NAEYC Young Children.* Retrieved from: www.naeyc.org/yc/files/yc/file/200203/Isbell_article _March_2002.pdf.

2. Schaper, R. C. (2017). Reading + reception = language development for preschoolers. Retrieved on April 10, 2017, from: www.michiganspeechhearing.org /docs/Schaper%20Reading%20and%20Repetition.pdf.

3. Schaper, 2017.

4. Biemiller, A., & Boote, C. (2006). An effective method for building meaning vocabulary in primary grades. *Journal of Educational Psychology, 98,* 44–62; Moschovaki, E., & Meadows, S. (2004). A short term longitudinal study of classroom book reading in Greek kindergarten schools. *Educational Studies in Language and Literature, 4,* 151–168.

5. Ard & Beverly, 2004; Walsh & Blewitt, 2006.

6. Talk More was modeled from the PEER prompt in dialogic reading; Lonigan & Whitehurst, 1998; Whitehurst et al., 1994.

CHAPTER 4

1. Gest, S. D., Holland-Coviello, R., Welsh, J. A., Eicher-Catt, D. L., & Gill, S. (2006). Language development subcontexts in Head Start classrooms: Distinctive patterns of teacher talk during free play, mealtime, and book reading. *Early Education and Development, 17,* 293–315.

2. Skibbe, L. E., Connor, C. M., Morrison, F. J., & Jewkes, A. M. (2011). Schooling effects on preschoolers' self-regulation, early literacy, and language growth. *Early Childhood Research Quarterly, 26,* 42–49.

3. Snowling, M., & Hulme, C. (Eds.). (2007). *The science of reading: A handbook.* Malden, MA: Blackwell Publishing, p. 207.

4. Perfetti, C. A., Landi, N., & Oakhill, J. (2007). The acquisition of reading comprehension skill. In M. Snowling & C. Hulme (Eds.), *The science of reading: A handbook* (pp. 209–226). Malden, MA: Blackwell Publishing.

5. Kintsch, W., & Rawson, K. A. (2007). Comprehension. In M. Snowling & C. Hulme (Eds.), *The science of reading: A handbook.* Malden, MA: Blackwell Publishing.

6. Kintsch & Rawson, 2007.

7. Perfetti et al., 2007.

8. Perfetti et al., 2007.

9. Whitehurst et al., 1994.

10. Perfetti et al., 2007.

11. Stein, N. L., & Albro, E. R. (1997). The emergence of narrative understanding: Evidence for rapid learning in personally relevant contexts. *Contemporary Issues in Education, 60,* 83–98.

12. Iowa Department of Education. (2006). *Every Child Reads. 3-5 Years Old.* Retrieved from: www.statelibraryofiowa.org/ld/t-z/youthservices/early-literacy-workshop-2014/retelling-stories-2.

13. Wasik, B. A., & Hindman, A. H. (2011). Improving vocabulary and pre-literacy skills of at-risk preschoolers through teacher professional development. *Journal of Educational Psychology, 103,* 455–469.

14. Wasik & Hindman, 2011.

15. Wasik & Hindman, 2011.

16. Wasik & Hindman, 2011.

17. Kintsch & Rawson, 2007, p. 219.

18. Perfetti et al., 2007.

CHAPTER 5

1. Ezell & Justice, 2005.

2. Muter, V., Hulme, C., Snowling, J. M., & Stevenson, J. (2004). Phonemes, rimes, vocabulary, and grammatical skills as foundations for early reading development: Evidence from a longitudinal study. *Developmental Psychology, 40,* 665–681; Senechal, M., & LeFevre, J. (2002). Parental involvement in the development of children's reading skill: A five-year longitudinal study. *Child Development, 73,* 445–460; Spira, E. G., Bracken, S. S., & Fischel, J. E. (2005). Predicting improvement after first-grade reading difficulties: The effects of oral language, emergent literacy, and behavior skills. *Developmental Psychology, 38,* 934–947; Storch, S. A., & Whitehurst, G. J. (2002). Oral language and code-related precursors to reading: Evidence from a longitudinal structural model. *Developmental Psychology, 38,* 934–947.

3. Cain, Oakhill, & Bryant, 2004; Nation, K., Clarke, P., Marshall, C. M., & Durand, M. (2004). Hidden language impairment in children: Parallels between poor

reading comprehension and specific language impairment? *Journal of Speech, Language, and Hearing Research, 47,* 199–211.

4. Biemiller, A. (2006). Vocabulary development and instruction: A prerequisite for school learning. In D. Dickinson, & S. B. Neuman (Eds.), *Handbook of early literacy research* (vol. 2, pp. 41–52). New York: Guilford Publishing.

5. Hart, B. & Risley, T. R. (1995). *Meaningful differences in the everyday experience of young American children.* Baltimore, MD: Brookes Publishing.

6. Hart & Risley, 1995.

7. Suskind, D. (September 30, 2015). Answer sheet: Why parents should talk a lot to their young kids and choose their words carefully. *The Washington Post.*

8. Crain-Thoreson, C., & Dale, P. S. (1992). Do early talkers become early readers? Linguistic precocity, preschool language, and emergent literacy. *Developmental Psychology, 28,* 421–429; Flouri, E., & Buchanan, A. (2004). Early father's and mother's involvement and child's later outcomes. *British Journal of Educational Psychology, 74,* 141–153.

9. Christian, K., Morrison, F. J., & Bryant, F. B. (1998). Predicting kindergarten academic skills: Interactions among child care, maternal education, and family literacy environments. *Early Childhood Research Quarterly, 13,* 501–521.

10. Payne, A., Whitehurst, G. J., & Angell, A. L. (1994). The role of home literacy environment in the development of language ability in preschool children from low-income families. *Early Childhood Research Quarterly, 9,* 427–440.

11. Blewitt, P., Rump, K. M., Shealy, S. E., & Cook, S. A. (2009). Shared book reading: When and how questions affect young children's word learning. *Journal of Educational Psychology, 101,* 294–304; Reese, E., & Cox, A. (1999). Quality of adult book reading affects children's emergent literacy. *Developmental Psychology, 35,* 20–28.

12. Blewitt et al., 2009.

13. Kim, J. (November 30, 2015). READ Charlotte: An Amazing I.D.E.A. Read Charlotte Keynote Address, University of North Carolina at Charlotte.

14. Elley, W. B. (1989). Vocabulary acquisition from listening to stories. *Reading Research Quarterly, 24,* 174–187.

15. Robbins, C., & Ehri, L. C. (1994). Reading storybooks to kindergarteners helps them learn new vocabulary words. *Journal of Educational Psychology, 86,* 54–64.

16. Hirsh-Pasek, K., Golinkoff, R., Hennon, E. A., & Macguire, M. J. (2004). Hybrid theories at the frontier of development psychology: The emergent coalition of word learning as a case in point. In D. G. Hall & S. R. Waxman (Eds.), *Weaving a lexicon* (pp. 173–204). Cambridge, MA: MIT Press.

17. Dickinson & Porche, 2011.

18. Walsh & Blewitt, 2006.

19. van Kleeck, Vander Woude, & Hammett, 2006.

20. Reese & Cox, 1999.

21. Reese & Cox, 1999; DeTemple, J., & Snow, C. E. (2003). Learning words from books. In A. van Kleeck, S. A. Stahl, & E. B. Bauer (Eds.), *On reading books to children: Parents and teachers* (pp. 271–319). Mahwah, NJ: Erlbaum Publishing; Pelligrini, A. D., Brody, G. H., & Sigel, I. E. (1985). Parents' book-reading habits with their children. *Journal of Educational Psychology, 77,* 332–340.

22. Roberts et al., 2005.

23. Wasik, B. A., & Bond, M. A. (2001). Beyond the pages of a book: Interactive book reading and language development in preschool classrooms. *Journal of Educational Psychology, 93,* 243–250.

24. Roberts et al., 2005.

CHAPTER 6

1. Cain, K., & Oakhill, J. V. (2007). Reading comprehension difficulties: Correlates, causes, and consequences. In K. Cain & J. Oakhill (Eds.), *Children's comprehension problems in oral and written language: A cognitive perspective* (pp. 41–70). New York: Guilford Press; Graesser, A., Golding, J. M., & Long, D. L. (1991). Narrative representation and comprehension. In R. Barr, M. L. Kamil, P. Mosenthal, & P. D. Pearson (Eds.), *Handbook of reading research* (vol. 2, pp. 171–205). White Plains, NY: Longman Publishing; Kendeou, P., van den Broek, P., White, M. J., & Lynch, J. S. (2007). Comprehension in preschool and early elementary children: Skill development and strategy intervention. In D. S. McNamara (Ed.), *Reading comprehension strategies: Theories, interventions, and techniques* (pp. 27–45). Hillsdale, NJ: Erlbaum Publishing.

2. Kendeou, P., van den Broek, P., White, M. J., & Lynch, J. S. (2009). Predicting reading comprehension in early elementary school: The independent contributions of oral language and decoding skills. *Journal of Educational Psychology, 101,* 765–778.

3. Mandler, J. M., & Goodman, J. S. (1982). On the psychological validity of story structure. *Journal of Verbal Learning and Verbal Behavior, 21,* 507–523.

4. Albers, P. (January 5, 2016). Why stories matter for children's learning. *The Conversation.* Retrieved from: www.theconversation.com/why-stories-matter-for-childrens-learning-52135.

5. Kaefer, Neuman, & Pinkham, 2015.

6. Elbro, C., & Buch-Iversen, I. (2013). Activation of background knowledge for inference-making: Effects on reading comprehension. *Scientific Studies of Reading, 17,* 435–452.

7. Recht, D., & Leslie, L. (1988). Effect of prior knowledge on good and poor readers' memory of text. *Journal of Educational Psychology, 80,* 16.

8. Kendeou et al., 2007.

9. Cain & Oakhill, 2007.

10. Neuman, S., Kaefer, T., & Pinkham, A. Building background knowledge. *Reading Rockets.* Retrieved January 22, 2018, from: www.readingrockets.org/article/building-background-knowledge.

11. Neuman et al., 2018.

12. Snowling & Hulme, 2007.

CHAPTER 7

1. National Reading Panel, 2000.

2. National Early Literacy Panel. (2008). *Developing early literacy: Report of the National Early Literacy Panel.* Retrieved from: lincs.ed.gov/publications/pdf/NELPR eport09.pdf.

3. Ukrainetz, T. A., Cooney, M. H., Dyer, S. K., Kysar, A. J., & Harris, T. J. (2000). An investigation into teaching phonemic awareness through shared reading and writing. *Early Childhood Research Quarterly, 15,* 331–355.

4. Ukrainetz et al., 2000.

5. Leppanen, U., Aunola, K., Niemi, P., & Nurmi, J. (2008). Letter knowledge predicts grade 4 reading fluency and reading comprehension. *Learning and Instruction, 18,* 548–564.

6. Ehri, L. C. (2007). Development of sight word reading: Phases and findings. In M. L. Snowling & C. Hulme (Eds.), *The science of reading: A handbook* (pp. 135–154). Malden, MA: Blackwell Publishing.

7. Ehri, 2007.

8. Ehri, 2007.

9. Ehri, 2007.

10. Ehri, 2007.

11. Ehri, L. C., Nunes S., Stahl, S., & Willows, D. (2001). Systematic phonics instruction helps students learn to read: Evidence from the National Reading Panel's meta-analysis. *Review of Educational Research, 71,* 393–447.

12. Ehri, 2007.

13. Cunningham, A. E., Perry, K. E., Stanovich, K., & Share, D. (2002). Orthographic learning during reading: Examining the role of self-teaching. *Journal of Experimental Child Psychology, 82,* 185–199; Ehri, 2007; Stuart, M., & Coltheart, M. (1988). Does reading develop in a sequence of stages? *Cognition, 30,* 139–181.

14. Ehri, 2007.

15. Ehri, 2007.

CHAPTER 8

1. Evans, M. D. R., Kelley, J., Sikora, J., & Trelman, D. J. (2010). Family scholarly culture and educational success: Books and schooling in 27 nations. *Research in Social Stratification and Mobility, 28,* 171–197.

2. McQuillan, J. (1998). *The literacy crisis: False claims, real solutions.* Portsmouth, NH: Heinemann Publishing.

3. Evans et al., 2010.

4. Serpell, R., Sonnenschein, S., Baker, L., & Ganapathy, H. (2002). Intimate culture of families and the early socialization of literacy. *Journal of Family Psychology, 16,* 391–405.

5. Lindsay, J. (August 2010). *Children's access to print materials and education-related outcomes: Findings from a meta-analytic review.* Naperville, IL: Learning Point Associates.

6. Krashen, S., Lee, S., & McQuillan, J. (2008). Is the library important? Multivariate studies at the national and international level. International Association of School Librarianship. Selected papers from the Annual Conference, 1–13.

7. National Center for Educational Statistics. (2015). *National assessment of educational progress.* U.S. Department of Education. Retrieved from: nces.ed.gov/nations reportcard.

8. NCES, 2015.

9. Evans et al., 2010.

10. Dickinson, D. K., & Neuman, S. B. (2006). *Handbook for early literacy research.* New York: Guilford Publishing.

11. Neuman, S. B. (1999). Books make a difference: A study of access to literacy. *Reading Research Quarterly, 34,* 286–301.

12. Teale, W. H., Yokota, J., & Martinez, M. (2008). The book matters: Evaluating and selecting what to read aloud to young children. In A. DeBruin-Parecki (Ed.), *Effective early literacy practice: Here's how, here's why* (pp. 101–121). Baltimore, MD: Brookes Publishing.

13. Hoffman, J. L., Teale, W. H., & Yokota, J. (2015). The book matters! Choosing complex narrative texts to support literacy discussion. *NAEYC Young Children, 70.* Retrieved from: www.naeyc.org/yc/article/the-book-matters.

14. Hoffman et al., 2015.

15. Donnella, L. (2017). People of color accounted for 22 percent of children's book characters in 2016. NPR. Retrieved from: www.npr.org/sections /codeswitch/2017/02/17/515792141/authors-and-illustrators-of-color-accounted -for-22-percent-of-childrens-books.

16. Schickedanz, J., & Collins, M. F. (2012). *So much more than the ABCs: The early phases of reading and writing.* Washington, DC: National Association for the Education of Young Children.

17. Sipe, L. R. (2007). *Storytime: Young children's literary understanding in the classroom.* Language and Literacy Series. New York: Teacher's College Press.

18. Hoffman et al., 2015.

19. Hoffman et al., 2015.

CHAPTER 9

1. Fielding-Barnsley, R., & Purdie, N. (2003). Early intervention in the home for children at risk of reading failure. *Support for Learning, 18,* 77–82; Hargrave, A. C., & Senechal, M. (2000). A book reading intervention with preschool children who have limited vocabularies: The benefits of regular and dialogic reading. *Early Childhood Research Quarterly, 15,* 75–90.

2. Fung et al., 2005.

3. Towson, J., Gallagher, P. A., & Bingham, G. E. (2016). Dialogic reading: Language and preliteracy outcomes for young children with disabilities. *Journal of Early Intervention, 38,* 230–246.

4. Huennekens, M. E., & Yaoying, X. (2016). Using dialogic reading to enhance emergent literacy skills of young dual language learners. *Early Child Development and Care, 186,* 324–340.

5. Ordonez, C. L., Carlo, M. S., Snow, C. E., & McLaughlin, B. (2002). Depth and breadth of vocabulary in two languages: Which vocabulary skills transfer? *Journal of Educational Psychology, 94,* 719–728.

6. Guernsey, L. (October 21, 2016). The beginning of the end of the screen time wars: The American Association of Pediatrics updates its guidelines for young kids—finally. *Slate.* Retrieved from: http://www.slate.com/articles/technology/future_tense/2016/10/the_american_academy_of_pediatrics_new_screen_time_guidelines.html.

7. Common Sense Media. (October 21, 2017). New research by Common Sense finds major spike in mobile media use and device ownership by children 0 to 8. Retrieved from: https://www.commonsensemedia.org/about-us/news/press-releases/new-research-by-common-sense-finds-major-spike-in-mobile-media-use-and#.

8. Strouse, G. A., & Ganea, P. A. (2017b). Toddlers' word learning and transfer from electronic and print books. *Journal of Experimental Child Psychology, 156,* 129–142.

9. Verhallen, M. J., and Bus, A. G. (2009). Video storybook reading as a remedy for vocabulary deficits: Outcomes and processes. *Journal of Education Research, 1,* 172–196.

10. Strouse, G. A., & Ganea, P. A. (2017a). Parent-toddler behavior and language differ when reading electronic and print picture books. *Frontiers in Psychology, 8,* 677.

11. Richter, A., and Courage, M. L. (2017). Comparing electronic and paper storybooks for preschoolers: Attention, engagement, and recall. *Journal of Applied Developmental Psychology, 48,* 92–102.

12. Strouse & Ganea, 2017a.

13. Strouse & Ganea, 2017a.

14. Takacs, Z. K., Swart, E. K., & Bus, A. G. (2014). Can the computer replace the adult for storybook reading? A meta-analysis on the effects of multimedia stories as compared to sharing print stories with an adult. *Frontiers in Psychology, 5.*

15. Moody, A. K., Justice, L. M., & Cabell, S. Q. (2010). Electronic versus traditional storybooks: Relative influence on preschool children's engagement and communication. *Journal of Early Childhood Literacy, 10,* 294–313.

16. Strouse & Ganea, 2017b.

17. Mims, C. (January 22, 2018). What if children should be spending more time with screens? *The Wall Street Journal.*

18. Arnold et al., 1994.

19. Whitehurst, G. J. (2002). Dialogic reading: An effective way to read to preschoolers. *Reading Rockets.* Retrieved January 17, 2018, from: www.readingrockets.org.

APPENDIX C

1. Read Charlotte uses fourth-grade reading proficiency on the National Assessment of Educational Progress for Charlotte-Mecklenburg Schools as a proxy for third-grade reading outcomes.

References

Adams, M. (1990). *Beginning to read: Thinking and learning about print*. Cambridge, MA: MIT Press.

Albers, P. (January 5, 2016). Why stories matter for children's learning. *The Conversation*. Retrieved from: www.theconversation.com/why-stories-matter-for-childrens -learning-52135.

Ard, L. M., & Beverly, B. L. (2004). Preschool word learning during joint book reading: Effect of adult questions and comments. *Communication Disorders Quarterly, 26,* 17–28.

Arnold, D. H., Lonigan, C., Whitehurst, G. J., & Epstein, J. N. (1994). Accelerating language development through picture book reading: Replication and extension to a videotape training format. *Journal of Educational Psychology, 86,* 235–243.

Arnold, D. H., Whitehurst, G. J., Epstein, J. N., Angell, A. L., Smith, M., & Fischel, J. E. (1994). A picture book reading intervention in day care and home for children from low-income families. *Developmental Psychology, 30,* 679–689.

Biemiller, A. (2006). Vocabulary development and instruction: A prerequisite for school learning. In D. Dickinson & S. B. Neuman (Eds.), *Handbook of early literacy research* (vol. 2, pp. 41–51). New York: Guilford Publishing.

Biemiller, A., & Boote, C. (2006). An effective method for building meaning vocabulary in primary grades. *Journal of Educational Psychology, 98,* 44–62.

Blewitt, P., Rump, K. M., Shealy, S. E., & Cook, S. A. (2009). Shared book reading: When and how questions affect young children's word learning. *Journal of Educational Psychology, 101,* 294–304.

Burgess, S. (1997). The role of shared reading in the development of phonological awareness: A longitudinal study of middle to upper class children. *Early Child Development and Care, 127/128,* 191–199.

Bus, A., & van Ijzendoorn, M. (1988). Mother-child interactions, attachment, and emerging literacy: A cross-sectional study. *Child Development, 59,* 1262–1272.

Cain, K. (1996). Story knowledge and comprehension skill. In C. Cornoldi & J. V. Oakhill (Eds.), *Reading comprehension difficulties: Processes and intervention* (pp. 167–192). Mahwah, NJ: Erlbaum.

Cain, K., & Oakhill, J. V. (2007). Reading comprehension difficulties: Correlates, causes, and consequences. In K. Cain & J. Oakhill (Eds.), *Children's comprehension problems in oral and written language: A cognitive perspective* (pp. 41–70). New York: Guilford Press.

Cain, K., Oakhill, J., & Bryant, P. (2004). Children's reading comprehension ability: Concurrent prediction by working memory, verbal ability, and component skills. *Journal of Educational Psychology, 96,* 31–42.

Cain, K., Oakhill, J., & Lemmon, K. (2004). Individual differences in the inference of word meanings from context: The influence of reading comprehension, vocabulary knowledge, and memory capacity. *Journal of Educational Psychology, 96,* 571–681.

Christian, K., Morrison, F. J., & Bryant, F. B. (1998). Predicting kindergarten academic skills: Interactions among child care, maternal education, and family literacy environments. *Early Childhood Research Quarterly, 13,* 501–521.

Common Sense Media. (October 21, 2017). New research by Common Sense finds major spike in mobile media use and device ownership by children 0 to 8. Retrieved from: www.commonsensemedia.org/about-us/news/press-releases/new -research-by-common-sense-finds-major-spike-in-mobile-media-use-and#.

Crain-Thoreson, C., & Dale, P. S. (1992). Do early talkers become early readers? Linguistic precocity, preschool language, and emergent literacy. *Development Psychology, 28,* 421–429.

Cunningham, A. E., Perry, K. E., Stanovich, K., & Share, D. (2002). Orthographic learning during reading: Examining the role of self-teaching. *Journal of Experimental Child Psychology, 82,* 185–199.

DeTemple, J., & Snow, C. E. (2003). Learning words from books. In A. van Kleeck, S. A. Stahl, & E. B. Bauer (Eds.), *On reading books to children: Parents and teachers* (pp. 271–319). Mahwah, NJ: Erlbaum Publishing.

Dickinson, D. K., & Neuman, S. B. (2006). *Handbook for early literacy research.* New York: Guilford Publishing.

Dickinson, D. K., & Porche, M. V. (2011). Relation between language experiences in preschool classrooms and children's kindergarten and fourth-grade language and reading abilities. *Child Development, 82,* 870–886.

Donnella, L. (2017). People of color accounted for 22 percent of children's books characters in 2016. NPR. Retrieved from: www.npr.org/sections /codeswitch/2017/02/17/515792141/authors-and-illustrators-of-color-accounted -for-22-percent-of-children-s-books.

Duncan, G. J., Claessens, A., Huston, A. C., Pagani, L. S., Engel, M., Sexton, H., et al. (2007). School readiness and later achievement. *Developmental Psychology, 43,* 1428–1446.

Ehri, L. C. (2007). Development of sight word reading: Phases and findings. In M. L. Snowling & C. Hulme (Eds.), *The science of reading: A handbook* (pp. 135–154). Malden, MA: Blackwell Publishing.

Ehri, L. C., Nunes, S., Stahl, S., & Willows, D. (2001). Systematic phonics instruction helps students learn to read: Evidence from the National Reading Panel's meta-analysis. *Review of Educational Research, 71*, 393–447.

Elbro, C., & Buch-Iversen, I. (2013). Activation of background knowledge for inference making: Effects on reading comprehension. *Scientific Studies of Reading, 17*, 435–452.

Elley, W. B. (1989). Vocabulary acquisition from listening to stories. *Reading Research Quarterly, 24*, 174–187.

Evans, M. D. R., Kelley, J., Sikora, J., & Treiman, D. J. (2010). Family scholarly culture and educational success: Books and schooling in 27 nations. *Research in Social Stratification and Mobility, 28*, 171–197.

Ezell, H., & Justice, L. M. (2005). *Shared storybook reading: Building young children's language and emergent literacy skills.* Baltimore, MD: Brookes Publishing.

Fenson, L., Dale, P. S., Reznik, J. S., Bates, E., Thal, D. J., et al. (1994). Variability in early communicative development. *Monographs of the Society for Research in Child Development, 59*, i–85.

Fielding-Barnsley, R., & Purdie, N. (2003). Early intervention in the home for children at risk of reading failure. *Support for Learning, 18*, 77–82.

Flouri, E., & Buchanan, A. (2004). Early father's and mother's involvement and child's later outcomes. *British Journal of Educational Psychology, 74*, 141–153.

Fung, P., Chow, B. W., & McBride-Chang, C. (2005). The impact of a dialogic reading program on deaf and hard-of-hearing kindergarten and early primary school-aged students in Hong Kong. *The Journal of Deaf Studies and Deaf Education, 10*, 82–95.

Gest, S. D., Holland-Coviello, R., Welsh, J. A., Eicher-Catt, D. L., & Gill, S. (2006). Language development subcontexts in Head Start classrooms: Distinctive patterns of teacher talk during free play, mealtime, and book reading. *Early Education and Development, 17*, 293–315.

Girolametto, L., & Weitzman, E. (2002). Responsiveness of childcare providers in interactions with toddlers and preschoolers. *Language, Speech, and Hearing Services in Schools, 33*, 268–281.

Godfield, B. A., & Reznick, J. S. (1990). Early lexical acquisition: Rate, content, and the vocabulary spurt. *Journal of Child Language, 17*, 177–183.

Graesser, A., Golding, J. M., & Long, D. L. (1991). Narrative representation and comprehension. In R. Barr, M. L. Kamil, P. Mosenthal, & P. D. Pearson (Eds.), *Handbook of reading research* (vol. 2, pp. 171–205). White Plains, NY: Longman Publishing.

Guernsey, L. (October 21, 2016). The beginning of the end of the screen time wars: The American Association of Pediatrics updates its guidelines for young kids—finally. *Slate.* Retrieved from: http://www.slate.com/articles/technology/future_tense/2016/10/the_american_academy_of_pediatrics_new_screen_time_guidelines.html.

Hargrave, A. C., & Senechal, M. (2000). A book reading intervention with preschool children who have limited vocabularies: The benefits of regular and dialogic reading. *Early Childhood Research Quarterly, 15*, 75–90.

Hart, B., & Risley, T. R. (1995). *Meaningful differences in the everyday experience of young American children*. Baltimore, MD: Brookes Publishing.

Hernandez, D. J. (April 2011). *Double jeopardy: How third-grade reading skills and poverty influence high school graduation*. Baltimore: Annie E. Casey Foundation. Retrieved September 8, 2016, from: www.aecf.org/resources/double-jeopardy/.

Hirsh-Pasek, K., Golinkoff, R., Hennon, E. A., & Macguire, M. J. (2004). Hybrid theories at the frontier of developmental psychology: The emergent coalition of word learning as a case in point. In D. G. Hall & S. R. Waxman (Eds.), *Weaving a lexicon* (pp. 173–204). Cambridge, MA: MIT Press.

Hoff-Ginsburg, E. (1991). Mother-child conversation in different social classes and communicative settings. *Child Development, 62*, 782–796.

Hoffman, J. L., Teale, W. H., & Yokota, J. (2015). The book matters! Choosing complex narrative texts to support literacy discussion. *NAEYC Young Children, 70*. Retrieved from: www.naeyc.org/yc/article/the-book-matters.

Huennekens, M. E., & Yaoying, X. (2016). Using dialogic reading to enhance emergent literacy skills of young dual language learners. *Early Child Development and Care, 186*, 324–340.

Iowa Department of Education. (2006). *Every Child Reads. 3-5 Years Old*. Retrieved from: www.statelibraryofiowa.org/ld/t-z/youthservices/early-literacy-workshop-2014/retelling-stories-2.

Isbell, R. T. (2002). Telling and retelling stories: Language and literacy. *NAEYC Young Children*. Retrieved from: www.naeyc.org/yc/files/yc/file/200203/Isbell_article_March_2002.pdf.

Justice, L., & Kaderavek, J. (2004). Embedded-explicit emergent literacy intervention: Background and description of approach. *Language, Speech, and Hearing Services in Schools, 35*, 201–211.

Justice, L. M., McGinty, A. S., Piasta, S. B., Kaderavek, J. N., & Fan, X. (2010). Print-focused read-alouds in preschool classrooms: Intervention effectiveness and moderators of child outcomes. *Language, Speech, and Hearing Services in Schools, 41*, 504–521.

Kaefer, T., Neuman, S. B., & Pinkham, A. M. (2015). Pre-existing background knowledge influences socioeconomic differences in preschoolers' word learning and comprehension. *Reading Psychology, 36*, 203–231.

Kendeou, P., van den Broek, P., White, M. J., & Lynch, J. S. (2007). Comprehension in preschool and early elementary children: Skill development and strategy intervention. In D. S. McNamara (Ed.), *Reading comprehension strategies: Theories, interventions, and techniques* (pp. 27–45). Hillsdale, NJ: Erlbaum Publishing.

———. (2009). Predicting reading comprehension in early elementary school: The independent contributions of oral language and decoding skills. *Journal of Educational Psychology, 101*, 765–778.

Kim, J. (November 30, 2015). READ Charlotte: An Amazing I.D.E.A. Read Charlotte Keynote Address, University of North Carolina at Charlotte.

Kintsch, W., & Rawson, K. A. (2007). Comprehension. In M. Snowling & C. Hulme (Eds.), *The science of reading: A handbook*. Malden, MA: Blackwell Publishing.

Krashen, S., Ley, S., & McQuillan, J. (2008). Is the library important? Multivariate studies at the national and international level. International Association of School Librarianship. Selected papers from the Annual Conference, 1–13.

Lefebvre, P., Trudeau, N., & Sutton, A. (2011). Enhancing vocabulary, print awareness, and phonological awareness through shared storybook reading with low-income preschoolers. *Journal of Early Childhood Literacy, 11,* 453–479.

Leppanen, U., Aunola, K., Niemi, P., & Nurmi, J. (2008). Letter knowledge predicts grade 4 reading fluency and reading comprehension. *Learning and Instruction, 18,* 548–564.

Leseman, P., & de Jong, P. G. (1998). Home literacy: Opportunity, instruction, cooperation, and social-emotional quality predicting early reading achievement. *Reading Research Quarterly, 33,* 294–318.

Leung, C. B. (2008). Preschoolers' acquisition of scientific vocabulary through repeated read-aloud events, retellings, and hands-on activities. *Reading Psychology, 29,* 165–193.

Lindsay, J. (August 2010). *Children's access to print materials and education related outcomes. Findings from a meta-analytic review.* Naperville, IL: Learning Point Associates.

Lonigan, C. J., Burgess, S. R., & Anthony, J. L. (2000). Development of emergent and early reading skills in preschool children: Evidence from latent-variable longitudinal study. *Developmental Psychology, 36,* 596–613.

Lonigan, C. J., & Whitehurst, G. J. (1998). Relative efficacy of parent and teacher involvement in a shared-reading intervention for preschool children from low-income backgrounds. *Early Childhood Research Quarterly, 13,* 263–290.

Mandler, J. M., & Goodman, J. S. (1982). On the psychological validity of story structure. *Journal of Verbal Learning and Verbal Behavior, 21,* 507–523.

McGinty, A. S., & Justice, L. M. (2009). Predictors of print knowledge in children with specific language impairment: Experiential and developmental factors. *Journal of Speech, Language, and Hearing Research, 52,* 81–97.

McQuillan, J. (1998). *The literacy crisis: False claims and real solutions.* Portsmouth, NH: Heinemann Publishing.

Mims, C. (January 22, 2018). What if children should be spending more time with screens? *The Wall Street Journal.*

Mol, S. E., Bus, A. G., & de Jong, M. T. (2009). Interactive book reading in early education: A tool to stimulate print knowledge as well as oral language. *Review of Educational Research, 79,* 979–1007.

Moody, A. K., Justice, L. M., & Cabell, S. Q. (2010). Electronic versus traditional storybooks: Relative influence on preschool children's engagement and communication. *Journal of Early Child Literacy, 10,* 294–313.

Moschovaki, E., & Meadows, S. (2004). A short term longitudinal study of classroom book reading in Greek kindergarten schools. *Educational Studies in Language and Literature, 4,* 151–168.

Muter, V., Hulme, C., Snowling, M. J., & Stevenson, J. (2004). Phonemes, rimes, vocabulary, and grammatical skills as foundations for early reading development: Evidence from a longitudinal study. *Developmental Psychology, 40,* 665–681.

Nation, K., Clarke, P., Marshall, C. M., & Durand, M. (2004). Hidden language impairments in children: Parallels between poor reading comprehension and specific language impairment? *Journal of Speech, Language, and Hearing Research, 47,* 199–211.

Nation, K., & Snowling, M. J. (2004). Beyond phonological skills: Broader language skills contribute to the development of reading. *Journal of Research in Reading, 27,* 342–356.

National Center for Educational Statistics. (2015). *National assessment of educational progress.* U.S. Department of Education. Retrieved from: nces.ed.gov/nationsreportcard.

National Early Literacy Panel. (2008). *Developing early literacy: Report of the National Early Literacy Panel.* Retrieved from: lincs.ed.gov/publications/pdf/NELPReport09.pdf.

National Institutes of Health. Speech and language developmental milestones. *Reading Rockets.* Retrieved April 10, 2017, from: www.readingrockets.org/article/speech-and-language-developmental-milestones.

National Reading Panel. (2000). *Report of the National Reading Panel: Teaching children to read: An evidence-based assessment of the scientific research literature on reading and its implications for reading instruction: Reports of the subgroups.* Washington, DC: National Institute of Child Health and Human Development, National Institutes of Health.

Neuman, S. B. (1999). Books make a difference: A study of access to literacy. *Reading Research Quarterly, 34,* 286–301.

Neuman, S., Kaefer, T., & Pinkham, A. Building background knowledge. *Reading Rockets.* Retrieved January 22, 2018, from: www.readingrockets.org/article/building-background-knowledge.

Ordonez, C. L., Carlo, M. S., Snow, C. E., & McLaughlin, B. (2002). Depth and breadth of vocabulary in two languages: Which vocabulary skills transfer? *Journal of Educational Psychology, 94,* 719–728.

Payne, A., Whitehurst, G. J., & Angell, A. L. (1994). The role of home literacy environment in the development of language ability in preschool children from low-income families. *Early Childhood Research Quarterly, 9,* 427–440.

Pelligrini, A. D., Brody, G. H., & Sigel, I. E. (1985). Parents' book-reading habits with their children. *Journal of Educational Psychology, 77,* 332–340.

Perfetti, C. A., Landi. N., & Oakhill, J. (2007). The acquisition of reading comprehension skill. In M. Snowling & C. Hulme (Eds.), *The science of reading: A handbook* (pp. 209–226). Malden, MA: Blackwell Publishing.

Phillips, G., & McNaughton, S. (1990). The practice of storybook reading to preschool children in mainstream New Zealand families. *Reading Research Quarterly, 25,* 196–212.

Rashen, S., Lee, S., & McQuillan, J. (2012). Is the library important? Multivariate studies at the national and international level. *Journal of Language and Literacy Education, 8.* Retrieved from: jolle.coe.uga.edu/wp-content/uploads/2012/06/Is-the-Library-Important.pdf.

Ravid, D., & Tolchinsky, L. (2002). Developing linguistic literacy: A comprehension model. *Journal of Child Language, 29,* 417–447.

Recht, D., & Leslie, L. (1988). Effect of print knowledge on good and poor readers' memory of text. *Journal of Educational Psychology, 80,* 16.

Reese, E., & Cox, A. (1999). Quality of adult book reading affects children's emergent literacy. *Developmental Psychology, 35,* 20–28.

Richter, A., and Courage, M. L. (2017). Comparing electronic and paper storybooks for preschoolers: Attention, engagement, and recall. *Journal of Applied Developmental Psychology, 48,* 92–102.

Robbins, C., & Ehri, L. C. (1994). Reading storybooks to kindergarteners helps them learn new vocabulary words. *Journal of Educational Psychology, 86,* 54–64.

Roberts, T. A. (2011). Preschool foundations for reading and writing success. In R. E. O'Connor & P. F. Vadasy (Eds.), *Handbook of reading interventions.* New York: Guildford Press.

Roberts, J., Jurgens, J., & Burchinal, M. (2005). The role of home literacy practices in preschool children's language and emergent literacy skills. *Journal of Speech, Language, and Hearing Research, 48,* 345–359.

Schaper, R. C. (2017). Reading + repetition = language development for preschoolers. Retrieved on April 10, 2017, from: www.michiganspeechhearing.org/docs /Schaper%20Reading%20and%20Repetition.pdf.

Schatschneider, C., Fletcher, J. M., Francis, D. J., Carbon, C. D., & Fourman, B. R. (2004). Kindergarten prediction of reading skills: A longitudinal comparative analysis. *Journal of Educational Psychology, 96,* 265–282.

Schickedanz, J., & Collins, M. F. (2012). *So much more than ABCs: The early phases of reading and writing.* Washington, DC: National Association for the Education of Young Children.

Senechal, M., & LeFevre, J. (2002). Parental involvement in the development of children's reading skill: A five-year longitudinal study. *Child Development, 73,* 445–460.

Senechal, M., Thomas, E., & Moner, J. A. (1995). Individual differences in 4-year-old children's acquisition of vocabulary during storybook reading. *Journal of Educational Psychology, 87,* 218–229.

Serpell, R., Sonnenschein, S., Baker, L., & Ganapathy, H. (2002). Intimate culture of families and the early socialization of literacy. *Journal of Family Psychology, 16,* 391–405.

Sipe, L. R. (2007). *Storytime: Young children's literary understanding in the classroom.* Language and Literacy Series. New York: Teachers College Press.

Skibbe, L. E., Connor, C. M., Morrison, F. J., & Jewkes, A. M. (2011). Schooling effects on preschoolers' self-regulation, early literacy, and language growth. *Early Childhood Research Quarterly, 26,* 42–49.

Snow, C. E., Burns, M. S., & Griffin, P. (Eds.). (1998). *Preventing reading difficulties in young children.* Washington, DC: National Academy Press.

Snowling, M., & Hulme, C. (Eds.). (2007). *The science of reading: A handbook.* Malden, MA: Blackwell Publishing.

Spira, E. G., Bracken, S. S., & Fischel, J. E. (2005). Predicting improvement after first-grade reading difficulties: The effects of oral language, emergent literacy, and behavior skills. *Developmental Psychology, 38,* 934–947.

Stanovich, K. E. (1986). Matthew effects in reading: Some consequences of individual differences in the acquisition of literacy. *Reading Research Quarterly, 21,* 360–406.

Stein, N. L., & Albro, E. R. (1997). The emergence of narrative understanding: Evidence for rapid learning in personally relevant contexts. *Contemporary Issues in Education, 60,* 83–98.

Storch, S. A., & Whitehurst, G. J. (2002). Oral language and code-related precursors to reading: Evidence from a longitudinal structural model. *Developmental Psychology, 38,* 934–947.

Strouse, G. A, & Ganea, P. A. (2017a). Parent-toddler behavior and language differ when reading electronic and print picture books. *Frontiers in Psychology, 8,* 677.

———. (2017b). Toddlers' word learning and transfer from electronic to print books. *Journal of Experimental Child Psychology, 156,* 129–142.

Stuart, M., & Coltheart, M. (1988). Does reading develop in a sequence of stages? *Cognition, 30,* 139–181.

Suskind, D. (September 30, 2015). Answer sheet: Why parents should talk a lot to their young kids and choose their words carefully. *The Washington Post.*

Takacs, Z. K., Swart, E. K., & Bus, A. G. (2014). Can the computer replace the adult for storybook reading? A meta-analysis on the effects of multimedia stories as compared to sharing print stories with an adult. *Frontiers in Psychology, 5.*

Teale, W. H., Yokota, J., & Martinez, M. (2008). The book matters: Evaluating and selecting what to read aloud to young children. In A. DeBruin-Parecki (Ed.), *Effective early literacy practice: Here's how, here's why* (pp. 101–121). Baltimore, MD: Brookes Publishing.

Tomasello, M., & Farrar, M. J. (1986). Joint attention and early language. *Child Development, 57,* 1454–1463.

Towson, J., Gallagher, P. A., & Bingham, G. E. (2016). Dialogic reading: Language and preliteracy outcomes for young children with disabilities. *Journal of Early Intervention, 38,* 230–246.

Ukrainetz, T. A., Cooney, M. H., Dyer, S. K., Kysar, A. J., & Harris, T. J. (2000). An investigation into teaching phonemic awareness through shared reading and writing. *Early Childhood Research Quarterly, 15,* 331–355.

University of Iowa. (August 3, 2007). Why do children experience a vocabulary explosion at 18 months of age? *Science Daily.* Retrieved from: www.sciencedaily.com /releases/2007/08/070802182054.htm.

Valdez-Menchaca, M. C., & Whitehurst, G. J. (1992). Accelerating language development through picture book reading: A systematic extension to Mexican day care. *Developmental Psychology, 28,* 1106–1114.

van Kleeck, A., Vander Woude, J., & Hammett, L. (2006). Fostering literal and inferential language skills in head start preschoolers with language impairment using scripted book sharing discussions. *American Journal of Speech-Language Pathology, 15,* 1–11.

Verhallen, M. J., & Bus, A. G. (2009). Video storybook reading as a remedy for vocabulary deficits: Outcomes and processes. *Journal of Education Research Online, 1,* 172–196.

Walsh, B. A., & Blewitt, P. (2006). The effect of questioning style during storybook reading on novel vocabulary acquisition of preschoolers. *Early Childhood Education Journal, 33,* 273–278.

Wasik, B. A., & Bond, M. A. (2001). Beyond the pages of a book: Interactive book reading and language development in preschool classrooms. *Journal of Educational Psychology, 93,* 243–250.

Wasik, B. A., Bond, M. A., & Hindman, A. (2006). The effects of a language and literacy intervention in Head Start children and teachers. *Journal of Educational Psychology, 98,* 63–74.

Wasik, B. A., & Hindman, A. H. (2011). Improving vocabulary and pre-literacy skills of at-risk preschoolers through teacher professional development. *Journal of Educational Psychology, 103,* 455–469.

Weizman, Z., & Snow, C. (2001). Lexical input as related to children's vocabulary acquisition: Effects of sophisticated exposure to support for meaning. *Developmental Psychology, 37,* 265–279.

Wells, G. (1985). *Language development in the preschool years.* New York: Cambridge University Press.

What Works Clearinghouse. (2010). *What Works Clearinghouse intervention report: Early childhood education intervention for children with disabilities: Dialogic reading.* Washington, DC: Institute for Education Sciences. Retrieved from: ies.ed.gov/ncee/wwc/interventionreport/136.

Whitehurst, G. J. (2002). Dialogic reading: An effective way to read to preschoolers. *Reading Rockets.* Retrieved January 17, 2018, from: www.readingrockets.org.

Whitehurst, G. J., Arnold, D. S., Epstein, J. N., Angell, A. L., Smith, M., & Fischel, J. E. (1994). A picture book reading intervention in day care and home for children from low-income families. *Developmental Psychology, 30,* 679–689.

Whitehurst, G. J., Falco, F. L., Lonigan, C. J., & Fischel, J. E. (1988). Accelerating language development through picture book reading. *Developmental Psychology, 24,* 552–559.

Zevenbergen, A. A., Worth, S., Pretto, D., & Travers, K. (2016). Parents' experiences in a home-based dialogic reading programme. *Early Childhood Development and Care,* 1–13.

About the Authors

Samantha Cleaver grew up in Chicago, Illinois. She taught special education and worked as an instructional coach before moving to Charlotte, North Carolina, where she led the initial design and startup of Active Reading work for Read Charlotte, a community-wide initiative to double the number of students reading on grade level by third grade in Mecklenburg County. She earned a doctorate in special education with a focus on literacy interventions from the University of North Carolina at Charlotte. Her favorite classic picture book is *Where the Wild Things Are* by Maurice Sendak, and she is currently reading *Jabari Jumps* by Gaia Cornwall to her two Active Readers.

Munro Richardson is the executive director of Read Charlotte, a community-wide initiative to double the number of students reading on grade level by third grade in Mecklenburg County, North Carolina. Richardson earned a doctorate from the University of Illinois at Urbana-Champaign in political science. He and his wife, Teresa, are the parents of three children, all of whom thankfully love books and reading. One of his favorite classic picture books is *The Snowy Day* by Ezra Jack Keats.